THE
BATTLE-TESTED
TEAMMATE

THE
BATTLE-TESTED
TEAMMATE

STORIES
AND PRINCIPLES
— TO —
IMPROVE YOURSELF
AND YOUR TEAM

BLAKE WILLIAMS

MOUNTAIN ARBOR
PRESS

MOUNTAIN ARBOR
PRESS
Alpharetta, GA

The author has tried to recreate events, locations, and conversations from his memories of them. The author has made every effort to give credit to the source of any images, quotes, or other material contained within and obtain permissions when feasible.

ISBN: 978-1-63183-684-8 - Paperback
eISBN: 978-1-63183-685-5 - ePub
eISBN: 978-1-63183-686-2 - mobi

Printed in the United States of America   1 2 2 3 1 9

♾This paper meets the requirements of ANSI/NISO Z39.48-1992 (Permanence of Paper)

For my home team: my beautiful wife, Hope, and my amazing kids, Cooper, Hadley, Hudson, Finley, and Everley. You are my reasons for working hard to become better.

CONTENTS

ACKNOWLEDGMENTS

So many people are part of my story, some of whom are mentioned in this book. Yet, there are plenty of other stories that make up my life, and lots of other people who played a role in those stories. I want to thank all of you who have played a role in my life. If you've played the part of mother, father, family, friend, adversary, coach, mentor, pastor, teacher, coworker, boss, employee, encourager, leader, follower—I thank you. In your own way, you have helped make me a better man. I'm also thankful for all of you who will continue to make me better in the stories to come.

INTRODUCTION

We all go through battles in life. I never felt very well-prepared for the battles I faced, be that as a student or as an adult. As much as being ill-prepared caused me to make mistakes, it also led me to creating Battle-Tested, a company that helps prepare student-athletes for the battles they'll face in life.

Student-athletes wouldn't want to go into a game situation unprepared for their opponent; they'd want to spend time preparing to increase their chances of success. They'd spend time training their bodies, learning the skills their sport requires, understanding their opponent, and hopefully training their minds for competition. Preparation builds confidence! So, in the same way, student-athletes should also prepare for the battles they'll face outside of sports in order to increase their chances to succeed in life. By preparing, they can be more confident when they find themselves in troubling times.

The intention of this book is to prepare you for the battles you'll face in your sport and in life.

Each chapter presents you with one principle you can apply to your life in order to become a better teammate. Not only can these principles make you a better teammate on your sports team, but they can make you better for the other teams you belong to: family, school, church, work, community, etc. If you're interested in becoming a more successful athlete in your sport, these principles can help with that, too.

As you read these stories, you may be reminded of a time in which you experienced something similar, and realize what your own story taught you or how it prepared you for life. If that happens, take time to think on your stories and how they impacted you; don't just rush ahead to the next chapter. Many of these stories will stir up emotions in you. I hope you'll take the time to figure out why.

WHY PRINCIPLES?

We need to live with principles in our life. Our principles serve as our own personal code of conduct. We need to let our principles dictate the majority of our decisions. If we don't, we leave our decision-making up to our feelings, which can often mislead us. Don't get me wrong; feelings are important, and we need to feel our feelings. But, if we allow our feelings to drive the majority of our choices and decisions, we hurt our chances of being successful. Let me give you an example.

A student-athlete is told by his or her coach to hit certain goals in the weight room or on the track prior to the start of the season. He or she has the entire summer to reach the goal. It's very likely that there'll be plenty of times during the long summer that the athlete doesn't *feel* like going to the gym; that they don't *feel* like going for that run; that they don't *feel* like eating the way they need to in order to reach the goal. If they wait to *feel* the right way before doing the right thing, it's highly likely they won't reach the desired goal.

However, if he or she lived by the right principles, the student-athlete's chances of reaching the goal skyrocket. The athlete may decide to live by the principle that he or she will always be known as one of the fittest members on the team. Maybe the athlete chooses to live by a principle that he or she will always be considered trustworthy by his or her coach and teammates. If the athlete choses to live by a principle like one of these, the principle should drive his or her behavior regardless of how the athlete might feel at the moment.

If you want to experience more success in your life, live by strong principles and let them drive your decisions much more than your feelings do. After all, your sport, your opponent, and your goals don't care about your feelings. If you want to dominate them, you need to dominate your feelings by living with strong principles.

I hope this book provides you with principles you'll apply to your team and to your life.

HOW TO READ THIS BOOK

One of my hopes with this book is that groups or teams of student-athletes will read through the book together, hopefully facilitated by their coaching staff. I've prepared questions for each chapter that coaches can download to help spark discussions between teammates. A team that takes the time to discuss the answers to these questions will not only get much more out of the book, they'll also develop deeper emotional connections to each other, which fosters greater trust—a vital need on any successful team.

If you do find yourself reading this book alone, I encourage you to take the time to think about how you might apply each chapter to help yourself become a better teammate. We all hear and gather a lot of information in our lives, but to be successful, we have to apply the things we learn. I don't just want this book to entertain you; I want the stories to lead you to implement these success principles in your life. Speed-reading this book will not help you do that. You need to take your time digesting each chapter, and then determine what actions you need to take to implement real, lasting change that can help you become a better version of yourself.

Download the discussion questions for the book here: iambattletested.com/teammate-book.

THE STORY BEFORE THE STORIES

I was born the youngest of four kids to my parents in a small hospital in Anniston, Alabama, in June 1970. My parents were married while in high school and started having children immediately. I have two older sisters: Kim, who is five years older than me, and Kerry, who was born two years after Kim. My older brother, Sammy, was born just thirteen months before me.

Also living under the same roof with us were my mom's parents and my mom's two younger brothers, Uncle Randy and Uncle Bob. For those not counting, that's ten of us living in one home. From what I am told, we lived in very modest conditions, moving from house to house when rent couldn't be paid.

Not long after I was born, my father started disappearing for long periods of time. So, he was largely absent in his marriage and in the lives of his kids. He'd tell me decades later that his job at a resale shop often got him in trouble because he'd buy and sell stolen property. This activity is a crime, and on more than one occasion my dad was arrested and put in jail. The sentences got longer with every arrest, thus the reason for his long absences.

Having a mostly absent husband put a lot of pressure on my young mother to try and take care of four kids. Her parents were both alcoholics and of little use in helping anybody but themselves, so my mom had to play mother to her two younger brothers, as well.

Although I was too young to remember much, my older siblings told me that our home was filled with various degrees of the following: alcoholism, drug use, guns, violence, abuse, neglect, and malnourishment.

I feel like I have genuine memories from my limited time with my birth family, but they could be fabricated based on stories Sammy told me as we grew up. I do have distinct memories of the day that the family split. I recall it being a nice day—short-and-T-shirt weather. I recall sitting inside a homemade fort made primarily of blankets that either my older siblings or, more likely, my uncles had built next to the trailer home we were living in at the time. My siblings and I were all in the fort playing when we heard Mom call for Sammy and me. We had visitors. It was my Great-Aunt Martha Williams (my dad's aunt) and her mother (my great-grandmother), Rena Mae Williams.

The next memory I have is of standing up in the back seat of a green four-door car (safety wasn't much of a concern back then) with Sammy as we headed to Martha's house in Talladega, Alabama, about thirty minutes away. Sammy and I had visited relatives before—in particular, one of my grandmothers who lived nearby and would babysit us often—but I remember this feeling different as I sucked my thumb in that back seat. It felt scary, lonely, and final. Over time, it did get less scary and less lonely, but it remained final.

CHAPTER 1

MY DAD MEMORY

I only have one childhood memory of my father. One. I can't recall my exact age when this memory happened, but my best guess is that I was somewhere between five and seven years old. I remember Martha hanging up the phone and telling me that my dad was coming to visit. Even though I had no previous memories of him, for some reason I was excited. I don't recall ever wondering where he'd been or why he'd never visited me before. I was just excited that he was coming to visit me now. It wouldn't be until years later that I'd find out my dad spent a fair amount of time in jail as I grew up.

I remember grabbing my baseball glove and ball and running into the yard to wait for him. It was a beautiful day for baseball, and as I waited for him, I threw the ball up into the air as high as I could and then tried to catch it, though I was usually unsuccessful. All the while I was thinking that surely when Dad arrived, he'd want to come play catch with me. I'd seen plenty of other neighborhood boys doing the same thing with their fathers. It's just one of those things that dads do with their boys.

After waiting for what seemed like forever, his car finally pulled into our driveway. He got out, greeted me, and told me he was going inside to talk to Martha and Mo (the nickname Sammy and I gave our great-grandmother). I waited outside, again throwing the ball up in the air and trying to catch it. After what seemed like only a few minutes, my dad came outside, but instead of playing with me, he said goodbye, got in his car, and left.

What just happened? I thought he was coming to play with me! He didn't throw me a single ball! Should I have asked him to? I just assumed that he would see in my face how badly I wanted him to play catch with me. He should have just known! Right? All dads are supposed to play catch with their boys!

I learned years later that my dad came to the house wanting to buy Mo's old antique car. My guess is he was probably looking for a quick flip to make some cash. When Mo told him the car wasn't for sale, he simply left. No time for a game of catch, apparently. Playing with me was not part of the reason for the visit.

While he was in jail, he couldn't spend time with me. When he got out of jail, he chose not to spend time with me.

LESSON

The events in this story, the only childhood memory I have of my father, delivered a very clear message to the boy standing in that yard with his ball and glove: you're not loveable; you're not wanted; an old car is more important than you. It's been over forty years since that day, and tears are falling as I write these words. But, the tears aren't for me. The tears aren't for the type of father I longed for. The tears are for that lonely little boy in the front yard and all the children like him. That little boy deserved better. He was loveable. He was wanted—maybe not by his dad, but by others. He was definitely worth more than any old car. He was worth a stinkin' game of catch!

Maybe you haven't experienced this exact same story in life, but chances are you have one very similar—maybe not similar in cause, but similar in the effect. It (whatever "it" was) happened to you, and it really hurt. It left you wounded and scarred. When it happened, your life changed, and perhaps from then on you began to question your worth on a regular basis. It caused you to clearly hear the voice in your head that devalues you, shames you, wraps you in chains, and shackles you to the floor, preventing you from straying too far from the safety of home base.

Some of you can't recall a specific situation that happened to you that caused you to hear the voices, but you still hear them, likely because of a lot of smaller events you experienced that, when added together, caused a similar effect.

As bad as others may have treated you, or as bad as the incidents were that happened to you, the voices in your head can hurt you far worse. Those voices can rob you of your potential and prevent you from really living life to its fullest.

This was true in my life for a long time. And really, it was my fault! I chose to listen to those negative voices in my head most of the time, long after I grew to be an adult. It really came down to choice. Was I going to choose to listen to the voices, or would I choose to ignore the voices that continually tried to hold me back from being my best?

Events happen in our lives, and they affect us. However, I truly believe that we determine how much we let them affect us. I let this "dad event" and other similar events (some you'll read about here) affect me in bad ways for too much of my life.

I hope you'll decide to not let your past drive you into a future you don't want.

TEAM APPLICATION

All coaches and teammates come with baggage. We've all been raised by imperfect people, which has made us imperfect, as well. Some of us may be very wounded from all the events we've faced in life. The current home life of coaches and teammates may also be very volatile. With this in mind, all team members need to be accepting and empathetic toward each other. Team gatherings should be a safe place for everyone. For some, being with the team may be a safer environment than they experience at home.

One of the best things a team can do to help foster acceptance and empathy is to openly share with each other. All team gatherings don't need to be about improving bodies, learning sports skills, mental training, and having fun. There needs to be time early on in the creation of a team when teammates can get to know each other on a deeper level, being vulnerable with each other about the events that have shaped who they are. As teammates better learn each other's stories, they can build empathy for each other, becoming more respectful, patient, and better equipped to help each other. Teammates might also realize they have more in common with each other than they thought, and form stronger and longer-lasting bonds with each other.

Principle:
The more we share, the more we care.

Sammy and me (standing) playing in the driveway.
Mo's car that my dad wanted to buy sits in the background.

CHAPTER 2

SIX FLAGS

When I was around eight years old, my mom, sisters, and a friend of one of my sisters pulled up to Martha's house in a big conversion van. I'd never been in a conversion van before. It was a mix of brown tones inside and out, and had thick carpeting on the floor. It was one of the vans where you could lay the back seat down flat to make a bed.

My mom had come to pick Sammy and me up for a day trip to Six Flags in Atlanta, Georgia, with our sisters. By this time, my mom had already moved to Florida, taking my sisters with her. I only have two specific memories from that day trip, but both were significant to me.

I remember my mom buying me a Pittsburgh Pirates batting helmet while we were there. It was bright-yellow plastic with a black bill and had a crisp, black letter P painted on the front. I grew up a big fan of the Atlanta Braves—mainly for geographic reasons—but the Pirates were winning a lot in the '70s, and I jumped on their bandwagon and rode it until another championship-winning team came along. I loved that helmet and used to wear it often, not just because I liked the Pirates, but likely because it was the only thing in my possession that my mom gave me.

The only other memory of that trip is of the ride home. I remember all of the kids sitting in the back of the van playing a game of hot potato with a ball. I recall having fun and everyone laughing. I also remember something inside pulling me away, like a little voice saying, "Don't enjoy yourself too much. It's only temporary. Don't get attached to these people, 'cause they're just going to leave you."

That voice caused me to pull away and sit alone in one of the captain's chairs, where I just stared out the window as we drove westbound toward Talladega along I-20. My siblings tried to get me to continue to play with them, but it was too late. I had put a barrier up to protect my heart, and it wasn't coming down. I wasn't going to get more emotionally invested in something that wasn't going to last. For the rest of the ride back to Martha's, I chose to stare out the window and count the mile markers as they passed.

Unfortunately, that voice inside of me was right. That day trip was like the last "big hurrah" for the Williams kids as a unit. Never again would we all be in the same place as kids. Sammy and I were left with Martha to remain as wards of the State of Alabama. It would be ten years before I'd see my mom or sisters again.

LESSON

Our wounds build walls around our hearts to protect us from future harm. When I began to have fun in that van ride home, it was like the wall of protection I'd built was being attacked. The temporary joy I was experiencing was trying to break down my wall. However, the wall won that day. It caused me to pull away and stare out the window in order to protect myself from the pain it knew I would feel when it came time to say goodbye.

Living a life with defenses always up, where you feel you can't trust others not to hurt you, is not a fun existence. It's like playing a waiting game where you know the bad ending is coming, but you don't know when, so the wall will make sure you're ready for it. You'll be able to bravely say, "I told you so," rather than crying in a heap. You'll walk cautiously through life, skeptical about the intentions and reliability of others. You're always on guard, like trying to tread carefully on the rocks around the edge of a lake so you don't fall in. There's a part of you that wants to just recklessly cannonball off the rocks into the lake, but that's too dangerous. You could get hurt. You're better off just hiding behind your wall.

There may be a season of life in which having a wall up to protect yourself is a good idea. But, just as seasons pass with time, there is likely a time when your wall needs to come down so you can experience life more fully. I could have kept my wall up with my mother for the rest of my life, but I would have missed out on the relationship we've been able to have that started in my college years. It hasn't been the easiest relationship, but I'm so thankful for my mother and the memories we've been able to make.

Walls cast shadows that we hide in. The sun doesn't shine in the shadows.

TEAM APPLICATION

Coaches and teammates are human and make mistakes that sometimes hurt us. When this happens, players can put walls up. Just as walls divide the rooms of a house, walls can also divide a team. A player who has been hurt may not even tell anyone that they've been hurt; they may just start building their wall. I've hurt people before who didn't tell me that I'd hurt them; they just started treating me differently all of a sudden.

A divided team will not function well, and they're also not much fun to be a part of. Rather than allowing hurt feelings to fester over mistakes that have been made, teammates need to speak openly when one feels they've been wronged by another so that the issue can be resolved quickly. Don't develop a long list of transgressions against a teammate and drop a bomb on them all at once. Clear the air as soon as possible after an incident happens. This can help a teammate address a behavior that might be hurting the team and that they might have been otherwise unaware of.

Principle:
I keep a clean slate with my teammates.

This is an old, blurry photo, but that's me on that day trip to Six Flags right after my mom bought me that batting helmet.

CHAPTER 3

CHIPMUNK

In August of 1978, I started the third grade. After second grade, the school I went to, Central School, closed. This meant that I'd attend Graham Elementary School on the opposite side of town. As you can imagine, there were fears about moving to a new school. Would I be liked? Would I be accepted? Would I make friends? I wasn't too sure how I'd adjust.

Luckily, I did have a few friends at Graham who I knew from attending the First United Methodist Church, something Martha made sure Sammy and I did regularly. My friends from church, like Howard O'Neal, Jim Adams, Dennis Gilliam, and Chris Cotter, all went to school at Graham. And, so did Susan. Ah, Susan! Who couldn't like Susan? Susan Syer was every bit as sweet and kind as she was beautiful in this third grader's eyes (and the eyes of many others, for sure).

Susan and I were both in Mrs. Monroe's class. I loved Mrs. Monroe! She was an older lady with short gray hair, big glasses, and a sweet personality. She was kind of like the grandmother anyone would want to have, and she was really great to me.

Even though I had known Susan through church to

some degree, I completely fell for her in Mrs. Monroe's third-grade class. I have a vivid memory of sitting in reading circle next to Susan in class one day, which I tried to do as much as possible. In my version of the story, she was wearing a white sundress worn off the shoulders that greatly complemented her summer tan (Susan claims she never had such a dress, but she can write her version of the story in her own book).

When it came her turn to read aloud from the book, something inside prompted me to put my arm around her. Maybe she was just an amazing reader, and I was so moved by her skills that I just had to display my feelings for her . . . or maybe I was just a dork . . . but I did it. And, I was glad I did! It was my way of sending a message to the other third-grade boys that she was mine.

Susan didn't move a muscle. She just kept reading like she was supposed to. She was unflappable! Maybe she felt sorry for the poor new kid. If so, I could be okay with that.

I can also vividly recall Valentine's Day in the third grade. Mrs. Monroe had taped a white paper bag for each student to the tray of the chalkboard in the front of the room. Each bag had a student's name written on it in big red letters. Mrs. Monroe called one student up at a time to place Valentine's cards for their classmates into the appropriate bags.

As I realized Mrs. Monroe's strategy, a lump formed in my throat and I began to sweat. I had spent all weekend working on a special Valentine's card for Susan. A store-bought card would not do! I mean, we're talking about Susan Syer here! I'd found a poem in a kid's journal that I thought spoke my feelings perfectly. I'm pretty sure it started with the words, "If I were a seabird, I'd fly to you." I had taken the time to copy it onto a big heart I had cut out of paper and colored in red ink. I had spent the better part of a day on this! And now, I was going to have to walk up to the chalkboard in front of the entire class, put normal store-bought cards in every other bag, but somehow try to get this oversized handmade heart into Susan's tiny bag. Gulp! But, guess what? I did it. And, I was glad I did! I think Susan may have blushed a little as the other kids laughed and pointed, but I was pretty happy with myself.

Later that spring, I was on the playground throwing a Frisbee with my friend Jim Adams. We were playing in the shade of huge oak trees on the playground. As we threw the Frisbee, a chipmunk ran between us to the safety of a fallen branch. As a goofy third-grade boy might do, I chased after it, knowing full well that there was no way I'd be able to get close to this chipmunk.

I was wrong.

As I ran up to the fallen branch, the chipmunk just sat there, almost as if he thought he was camouflaged and I couldn't see him. I slowly reached my right hand down through the twigs of the branch and picked him up. *No way! I caught a chipmunk! How cool is this?* I heard Jim say, "Let's go show Mrs. Monroe!" In the speed of a nanosecond, I processed the following thoughts: *Now, Jim. This is a quite the opportunity we have here. Yes, we could surely go and show sweet Mrs. Monroe, my favorite teacher, my skill at catching small rodents. I'm sure she'd be impressed. Or, I could take this opportunity to share the labor of my hard work with the one whose opinion I value much more than Mrs. Monroe.*

So, of course, I replied, "Nah. Let's go show Susan!"

Jim and I quickly found Susan on the playground. As I approached her with rodent in hand, her response was exactly what I was hoping for: "Aww. What a cute chipmunk!" As I heard those words, I thought, *This might pay off more than that Valentine's card!*

Susan began to pet the top of the chipmunk's head gently with one finger. When she did that, I could feel the chipmunk try to wiggle out of my right hand. I felt like I was going to drop him, so I used my left hand to pop him upward on his bottom, just a bit, so I could regain a good grip on him with my right hand. Well, when I did that, this dumb chipmunk bit down onto the tip of my middle finger . . . and didn't let go!

I pointed my right hand to the sky and fiercely slung it downward, dislodging the chipmunk from my finger and slamming it to the ground (killing it, I found out later). Warm blood now flowed down my hand and forearm, and I began crying like a newborn baby. I'm sure I was losing the credibility as a hunter I had built up with Susan faster than I was losing blood. And then, in that moment, I thought Jim's idea to go show Mrs. Monroe was great advice.

LESSON

Although this is a story I remember fondly and laugh about, it can teach a lesson. On the playground that day, I rushed into something without putting a whole lot of thought into it. I was no hunter. I was no wild-game chipmunk expert. Are there any dangers in catching a chipmunk? What would I do with it if I caught it? I simply saw the chipmunk and reacted without thinking.

Once I caught the chipmunk, Jim actually offered me sound advice for a third grader: "Let's go show Mrs. Monroe." I can only imagine that if I had gone to Mrs. Monroe with a chipmunk in hand, she likely would have yelled for me to drop it immediately, which I would have done (without getting bit). But, I let my pride in my accomplishment and my desire to brag blind me to the wisdom that Jim offered.

Our pride often tricks us into thinking we know what's best for us ("Impress Susan!"), even when the world around us is telling us something to the contrary ("Don't pick up a wild animal."). If only there were an "easy" button for life that we could press to get the right answer before we make our choices, or maybe at least a "pause" button so we would have more time to think about the pros and cons for a decision we're about to make (and maybe we'd even seek out the wisdom of others).

I think everyone would agree that we don't know it all, but there are many of us who think we know what's best for us. As we grow up, we so often ignore the wisdom shared by our parents or guardians, teachers, coaches, pastors, or elders. Despite our lack of experience, we think we know what's best, and we ignore wisdom of those who have journeyed through life much longer than we have. There's such wisdom gained in the journey! Unfortunately, choosing to ignore wisdom can come back to bite us—literally (like that chipmunk)! We need to humble ourselves much more than most of us usually do, and be willing to listen to those around us who have our best interests in mind.

If only it had taken a single chipmunk bite to fully teach me this lesson.

TEAM APPLICATION

There'll be plenty of student-athletes reading this book who believe they know more than their coach does. I've been around long enough to know what it looks like. They make comments to their family and friends about what an idiot their coach is. They use a mistake made by their coach as a reason for why they won't listen to them. They openly defy their coach's instructions because they think they know the best play to run. In practice, they coach their teammates on a "better way" to do things rather than the way coach instructed. I'd bet money that these players have family members at home who feed into their misguided beliefs.

Only once in almost five decades have I seen a coach who knew less about the game than the players did. It was when my oldest son was eight, and none of the dads could make the time to coach the team, so one of the moms agreed to coach as best she could. No, she didn't initially know if the home team batted first or last in the inning, but at least she was willing to fill the void. If someone earns the title of "Coach" (especially at high-school level and above), they almost always know more about the sport than the players they coach. They've certainly earned the right to be listened to.

One of the characteristics that college coaches most look for in their recruits is for a student-athlete to be coachable. Being coachable is the ability to easily take instruction from a coach in order to improve. If a player thinks he or she knows more than a coach does, how coachable is that player? Not very, because he or she doesn't think the coach offers any real value to him or her as a player. In order for a player to be coachable, he or she must first have humility. Without humility, that student-athlete won't be very willing to accept coaching from anyone, coach included.

Principle:
My humility drives my coachability.

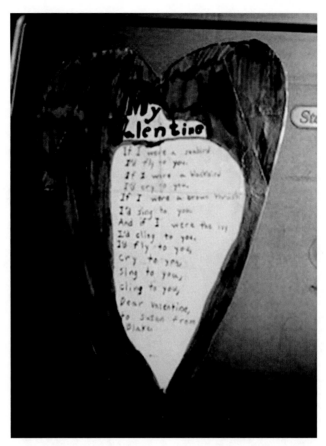

I made this Valentine card for Susan in the third grade.
She had it laminated and has kept it all these years.

CHAPTER 4

STUCK IN A TREE

As we grew up, one of the things that Sammy and I liked to do most was climb trees. Climbing a tree felt a lot like exploring unchartered territory. We had a great climbing tree in our front yard (an oak) that we spent a lot of time in. This oak had three different forks that split off into three different directions just above ground level, so it provided good climbing variety. Our Aunt Martha had someone help her hang a tire swing from one of the lower forks, and we played on it often. But, since Sammy and I liked to climb high, we spent most of our time on the tallest fork of the tree.

One day, Sammy and I decided to climb on the one fork of the oak that we'd never climbed out onto before. We'd never climbed on it because it looked pretty boring. There wasn't much to it. It rose from the ground and then bent at an almost ninety-degree angle over our driveway at a height of maybe fifteen feet. It didn't have many branches at all until its very end. But, for some reason that day, this fork was going to be conquered by the Williams brothers, tree climbers extraordinaire!

Sammy offered me the opportunity to play lead in the climb. In hindsight, maybe he knew something I didn't, but I happily obliged. When we reached the part of the fork where it began to run parallel to the ground below, there were no branches to hold onto. We'd have to bear-hug the limb and inch-worm our way out across it. It was a slow process, but it worked. As I got a few feet out onto the limb, I came face to face with a single branch sticking straight up. I tried breaking it to get it out of my way, but it was too thick. If we were going to conquer this fork, our only hope was to try to go around it.

I inched forward slowly, reached around the vertical branch, grabbed onto the limb on the other side, and tried to slowly inch myself around the branch. I looked down and saw the cement driveway staring back at me, as if to say, "Don't worry. I gotcha!" Someway, somehow, I was able to get around the branch, but in doing so, the weight of my legs nearly pulled me off the limb and onto the driveway below.

I was now safely on the other side of the branch with all body parts on the limb, bear-hugging it. The near-fall scared me to death. I quickly realized I was in trouble. I yelled, "Sammy, I'm stuck!"

"What do you mean, you're stuck? Just climb back," he said.

"I can't get back around that branch going backward. I'm stuck! Go get Martha!" I began to cry. Sammy could tell I was scared, and so he climbed down and ran in the house to get Martha. Martha was in her fifties, but somehow I hoped she'd be able to climb that tree and get me down.

Martha came out quickly to see what was going on. She could see the terror in my eyes and my four limbs in a death grip around the tree limb. She tried to coach me back down, but soon realized I wasn't moving anywhere. When you have a near-death experience, like I thought I had just had, there's a tendency to freeze up, which I did.

There's a lot of great things about growing up in a neighborhood with a lot of kids your age. The best part is that there's always someone around to play with. The bad part about growing up in such a neighborhood is that a boy stuck in a tree makes for great entertainment for the other kids. Before I knew it, neighbors were coming out of the woodworks to see what everyone was staring at up in this tree, and what the awful noise was coming down out of it! Since my panic was preventing me from coming down on my own, I really left Martha with no other options. She was forced to call the fire department.

When a fire truck pulls up into a crowded neighborhood in small town Alabama, even more neighbors have to come out to see what all the commotion is about. In hindsight, I bet Martha wished she'd have charged admission that day. She would've made good money for the show I was putting on!

A fireman grabbed an extension ladder and propped it up against the limb I was bear-hugging. He climbed up to me and said, "I gotcha, little man." I thought, *And you are . . . ?* This complete stranger was expecting me to let go of the bond I'd formed with this limb and trust him to get me out of this tree. That proved to be no easy task for him or me.

The thing is, I knew that as long as I bear-hugged that tree, I was safe. I wasn't going to fall; I controlled that. Surely, I could adapt to life in a tree over time. They could bring me a little food and water once in a while, maybe a blanket on cold nights. *Kind of like taking care of a baby bird*, I thought. *There's far worse ways to live life.* But as more neighbors gathered around and more kids pointed and laughed, I knew I was going to have to come down out of that tree and end the embarrassment. I mean, even if the fireman were to drop me onto the driveway below, my embarrassment would be over one way or another.

The fireman was eventually able to pry me off that limb (much like they do cats, I imagine) and bring me safely to the driveway below. As soon as my feet hit the pavement, I bolted into the house to get away from the cheering crowd. That's right, I never even stopped to thank the fireman. I didn't plan on showing my face again for years, and selfishly hoped some other kid in my neighborhood would get stuck in a tree. Misery loves company.

LESSON

Finding yourself out on a limb too afraid to make the next move is never a good place to be. Sure, I could have stayed there for a long while, too paralyzed to move, but there was no quality of life out on that limb. There was no joy. There was fear, doubt, misery, and more trouble. I couldn't get myself safely down off that limb on my own; I was stuck. There were only two ways down. One involved me crashing to the driveway below, and the other required me to let go and put my trust in someone else. Both options scared me to death.

I've had plenty of practice getting myself into tough situations—and sometimes getting myself out of them—all on my own. Even though I find myself in bad situations, if I hold on tightly enough, then I'm still in control of not falling, of not allowing things to get any worse, of turning things around. I feel safer when I'm in control. Letting go and allowing someone else to take control can make many of us very uneasy.

Many of us have been conditioned to think that needing

help from others is a sign of weakness. We've been taught to go out and show the world what we can do, and if you have to step on others to do it, so be it.

Asking for help is *not* a sign of weakness. Admitting you need help and asking for it requires both wisdom and courage.

Maybe you are currently out on a metaphorical limb of some sort. You're dangerously close to falling. You're keeping it together just enough that you're able to hold on . . . for now. How long can you keep it up? How long before you fall? How long will it be until you realize you have to rely on someone else for help? You may be able to do a lot of things alone, but why should you? Things are so much easier when we have help from others. There are people who love you and may just be waiting for you to ask them for help. They have the skills to help you where you may need it most. You also have a God who loves you and wants to help you. But, you first have to "let go of that limb" and allow someone to help you.

TEAM APPLICATION

I've seen plenty of student-athletes try to do things on their own. Maybe they want to prove to themselves or others that they don't need help. Maybe they have too much pride to ask for help. Maybe they don't trust that their teammates can help them. I've watched them struggle in these moments. Some may actually be able to accomplish the task alone, but all of us around them could see how much more easily the task could have been completed if they'd allowed their teammates to help.

Letting go of the need to go it alone is a must for a student-athlete.

Principle:
I must trust my teammates to do their job.

Martha and me posing in the same oak tree
that I'd later get stuck in.

CHAPTER 5

JIMBO

I played baseball until I reached the end of my middle school years. I wasn't a great player, certainly not good enough to play for my high school team (hence why baseball ended for me after middle school). The highlights of my baseball career are few, and occurred mostly in my Little League years. And, what I call "highlights" would likely not be considered highlights by anyone else.

In fact, most of my baseball memories are lowlights. Those lowlights are filled with me striking out time after time, playing a lot of right field, and crying in the bathtub after another game where I felt I had let my team down. Looking back on it, I'm honestly not sure why I continued to play year after year. Maybe I was always hopeful that the following year would be "my year." It never happened.

My first year of Little League was miserable. I was drafted to play on a team that was coached by the father of my friend Mike Hughston, who lived up the street from me and was one of the stars on the team. I always guessed I was drafted as a favor to Martha, certainly not because of my baseball skills. Without a dad to help me practice, and with a brother disinterested in baseball, I didn't have a lot of opportunities to practice fielding and hitting outside of scheduled team practices.

The good news is that we had a pretty good team that year led by Mike and some other good players who were a couple years older, more skilled, and more physically developed than me. The bad news is that every player had to play in every game. I hated that rule. I was content to sit on the bench and cheer my teammates on to victory. Yet, in every game I'd eventually get sent into right field, where I prayed no ball would be hit to me. Smart Little League coaches put their worst fielders in right field. But, the ball seems to have a way of finding players like me who stink at catching the ball. It seems every game I'd make an error that hurt my team, even though I didn't play much.

I'd usually end up batting at least once per game, as well. The only thing worse than my fielding was my hitting. My batting skills made me look like a gold-glove player in the field. I couldn't hit to save my life! I was so afraid of getting hit by the ball. I was one of those players who went to bat hoping the opposing pitcher would walk me. I was even coached to crouch down really low to make my strike zone smaller than it already was. I was either going to get walked or get struck out; it was all up to the pitcher. Sadly, I struck out an awful lot, again hurting my team. Nights after games where I'd struck out were the worst for me, and always led to a lot of tears in the postgame bath.

Despite the misery of my first year of Little League, I went back for a second year. After very limited success, I chose to play in my third and final year, as well. When you reach your third year of Little League, you're pretty much expected to play a bigger role, which of course was a concern for me, but at the same time exciting. I got to pitch some during that season, which was fairly fun. I didn't throw that hard, but I threw strikes fairly consistently, which at least gave the fielders behind me a chance to make plays.

In one game that season I found myself again in right field. The starting pitcher was a good friend and classmate of mine. Like many summer nights in Alabama, it was hot and humid. My friend was not having a great game pitching, and the other team was scoring a lot of runs against us. I was getting angry out in right field—not at my friend, but at the situation. I really wanted to go in and pitch to try to stop the bleeding, as they say. After a couple of innings, the coach actually called me in to pitch in relief. Excited and jogging in from right field, I felt like a Major League player coming in from the bullpen.

When I reached the mound, the coach wished me good luck. He knew as well as I did that I was going to need it. I took my allotted number of warm-up pitches and prepared to face my first batter under the bright lights. That's when something very surprising happened.

I heard a male voice yell from the crowd on the third-base side, "Come on, Blake!" It wasn't a voice I recognized. I didn't usually have people cheering for me. If I did, it was Martha or some other mom who felt sorry for me. This was a guy's voice. I'd always secretly hoped that one day I'd look over and see my dad in the crowd cheering for me. I never did, despite the fact that he only lived thirty minutes away (when he wasn't in jail).

The cheer came from Jimbo Knight. Jimbo stood on the other side of the chain-link fence along the third-base line. I knew of Jimbo, but I'm not sure how Jimbo knew of me. Jimbo was an amazing athlete growing up, especially on the football field. I'm pretty sure he even went on to play in college. I don't believe I'd ever even had a conversation with Jimbo before this point, though, and I'm not sure I ever had one with him afterward. Jimbo was a year older than me, and we ran in very different circles. I'm not sure why he was even attending a Little League game, but that didn't matter. What mattered was that *the* Jimbo Knight was at the game, and he was cheering for me!

All of a sudden, I felt ten feet tall and bullet proof as I climbed the pitcher's mound to throw my first pitch. Jimbo's encouragement made me want to rear back and throw extra hard. And, I did! The only problem was that my version of extra hard was still very hittable for the other team. They began to tee off on me just like they had my friend who had started the game.

Interestingly, Jimbo kept cheering for me, even when it appeared not to be doing any good, as I gave up hit after hit in a game my team would eventually lose. Jimbo never gave up on me that night; he just kept cheering for me for some reason. His voice didn't magically make me a better baseball player, but it inspired me to give the game everything I had. I left the field that night without regrets and feeling really good about myself, because I gave the best effort I could.

So, this serves as my favorite memory of my three seasons of Little League baseball. I doubt many other players would likely remember such a game as a highlight, but for me, it was unforgettable.

LESSON

The world needs more Jimbos, doesn't it? That night, Jimbo believed in me, or at least really acted like he did. Maybe he saw something in me that I didn't see in myself. Maybe there was potential that somehow he recognized that I'd never chosen to see or believe.

We all need someone to believe in us and cheer us on.

Because of my lack of belief in myself, I really needed a Jimbo in my life (I could have used an army of them, actually); and I needed a Jimbo for much more than that one night on that pitcher's mound. I needed someone I looked up to who would convey to me that they believed that I had what it took. I knew Martha believed in me, and knowing that was great. But as kids, the words of our parents or guardians can fall flat, simply because we feel that our family members are *supposed* to say nice things to and about us. There's something much more powerful when someone we admire who isn't close family, and maybe who doesn't know us like a family member would, says words to affirm us. When we hear those words from the right person, it can be like hearing those words for the first time—and they are so powerful. Having Jimbos around us helps inspire us to give greater effort and have greater belief in ourselves.

TEAM APPLICATION

We hold such power in our voices. You've likely been absolutely devastated by the powerful negative words of someone, and hopefully you've experienced the power of positive, life-giving words in your life. In Battle-Tested events I've led, I've seen the power of encouragement time and time again. I've seen loud shouts of encouragement toward an individual propel that person across a finish line they doubted they could reach. I've seen shouts of encouragement cause a person to summon strength they didn't know they had so their team could be successful. I've seen the power of encouragement compel many to overcome their fear and self-doubt.

Imagine if you had your own private cheering section that followed you around throughout the day. Do you think you'd get more things done? Do you think you'd give greater effort to the things you've committed to? Of course you would! Imagine how much better you might clean your room, brush your teeth, do the dishes, work out, do homework, practice, etc. if only you could hire traveling cheering sections (might not be a bad business to consider starting).

Until the day we can have our own cheering section follow us around, I recommend to teams that I work with to be the encouraging voices for each other. You should go out of your way to encourage those around you, to lend them the power you have in your voice. The more you choose to do that for others, the more likely they will do that for you in return.

I know plenty who will respond with the excuse, "I'm really shy, quiet, and just can't vocally encourage my teammates like that." This excuse is just that—an excuse. Being on a team is not about you nearly as much as it is about the team. You should be asking, "What does my team need from me?" If they need you to encourage them, which most do, you need to find a way to do it, not find an excuse why you can't. And, if someone tells me that it's just not comfortable for them to speak words of encouragement, I say, "I understand. Do it anyway." This is not about you being comfortable; it's about what others need from you. By now you should know that I'm all for you getting uncomfortable so that you can experience personal growth.

Principle:
I will be a Jimbo for my teammates.

Me in my first year of Little League baseball

CHAPTER 6

VICKI

One of the kids in my neighborhood that I spent a fair amount of time with as I grew up was a boy named Keith Allen. He was a year younger than I was, but probably more popular throughout middle school and high school. Keith and I were on the same peewee football team, but football stuck for him and he played all throughout high school.

Keith and I liked to ride bikes together in our middle school years, often riding through the woods or into other neighborhoods. On one particular sunny afternoon, Keith and I rode our bikes about a mile from home to where a number of my friends lived. As we rode along Shady Lane Circle, I could see we were approaching two young girls walking our way. One girl was my friend Vicki Luker, who was my age. I didn't know the other girl. Still some distance away from them and out of earshot, Keith said to me, "Oooh. I heard Vicki likes you."

Keith wasn't talking about "like" in the sense that Vicki considered me a good friend. In those middle school days, when someone "liked" you, it meant they were interested in you as something more than a friend. Now, as I said, Vicki was a good friend of mine, and she was cute, but I didn't "like" her like that. And, chances are she didn't "like" me like that, either. Keith was probably just trying to stir the pot to see what bubbled up. Either way, I found Keith's comment embarrassing. I felt this strong desire to let Keith know that I didn't "like" Vicki.

As we pedaled close to Vicki and her friend, Vicki said, "Hi, Blake," to which I replied, "Hi, bitch," while passing her on my bike.

There, that should do it. It should be crystal clear now to Keith that I don't "like" Vicki.

Keith reeled with glee, showing his full support for my comment. I immediately had some mixed emotions about what I'd done, but mostly the middle school boy in me was pleased with what I'd said. The last thing I wanted were rumors going around school about me "liking" someone that I didn't, and being laughed at as a result. Middle school kids can be ruthless with those kinds of things.

I lived less than a mile from where the name-calling incident took place. By the time I got home and walked in the door, Martha already knew what I'd done. Word travels fast in a small town, but my friends and I used to refer to Martha as the "hound-dog" (in a loving way, of course). If Sammy or I did anything wrong, she was going to find out about it. She was so well-networked in Talladega, it was like she had spies placed all around town to quickly report any news, good or bad, about the Williams boys.

As soon as I walked in the house, the look on Martha's face showed trouble. She asked, "What did you say to Vicki?"

Of course, she already knew what I had said to Vicki, but I guess she wanted to see if I'd come clean or tell a lie. Any belief that I'd made a good decision speaking to Vicki the way that I had left my body instantly. Apparently, Vicki had gone straight home after our encounter, crying as she told her mother about what had happened. Her mom, of course, called Martha (she must have been in the spy network).

Besides getting grounded, I received the worst punishment I could have thought possible in the moment. Martha made me call Vicki's house and apologize to both Vicki and her mom. Ugh! I knew I had made a huge mistake, but couldn't we all just forget about it? Couldn't I send her a letter instead?

That phone call was really hard to make, largely because I was crying so much it was hard to speak clearly, but also because I had hurt a friend of mine . . . and her mom. All because I caved into the pressure I felt to be "cool" and win Keith's respect.

Thankfully, both Vicki and her mom accepted my apology that day. Vicki and I remained good friends throughout middle and high school. I even spent some time in groups at her house, and her mom never made me feel anything other than welcomed. Their forgiveness was real.

At our ten-year high school reunion, I mentioned this story to Vicki and expressed my remorse again. And you know what? Vicki claimed to have no memory of it! Something that impacted me so deeply was not even a blip on her radar. She was not only able to forgive, but also able to forget.

LESSON

On that day, I sought Keith's acceptance and approval, and I was willing to hurt someone else (a friend) in order to get it. Although much worse, it does make me wonder about some would-be gang members who are asked to perform violent acts on others in order to get accepted into the gang. Who they hurt doesn't matter to them, at least not near as much as winning the approval of the gang.

My need to feel accepted by Keith in that moment was directly related to the wounds I'd received years earlier when the family split up and I had felt abandoned. I desperately sought the acceptance of others for many years because I felt like I must be unlovable in some way. I was letting my history be my enemy instead of my ally.

TEAM APPLICATION

Many athletes allow their history to be their enemy. We see it in all levels of sports. We see it when a player has a bad at-bat, and they let it carry over to the next at-bat, the next time they get the ball, or in the next game. We see it when a player makes a mistake that costs their team in some way, and they let that recent history prevent them from being a good teammate or being effective in their role for the rest of the game. We see it when a player is the victim of a cheap shot and later in the game gets penalized when they seek retaliation. They are being dominated by their history.

The most successful athletes are those who have learned to let their history be their friend. We know that all athletes make mistakes, but the best learn from their history to help them in the future. They're able to gain wisdom from their mistakes so they can be more successful in their next attempt. They accept that the past mistakes don't define their worth, and they simply work to get better.

It's normal for automatic negative thoughts to creep in

when we fail or make mistakes. We hear "You stink!" in our heads. To be our best for our team, we have to make a conscious decision to ignore that voice and listen to what our history wants to teach us.

Principle:
I allow my history to be my ally, not my enemy.

CHAPTER 7

MIDDLE SCHOOL BULLY

I was one of the shortest kids in my class during middle school. I was 4'11" for what seemed like years. I remember having Martha measure me all the time, only to hear back, "Not quite five feet yet." I longed to be tall. I felt that if I were only taller, like so many others in my school, then I'd be stronger, more popular, more respected, and less of a target for the bullies.

My physical development was directly opposite of my brother Sammy. Sammy matured very quickly and was one of the strongest, baddest dudes in middle school. He was a tough guy. He was somewhat of a bully, too, and not just toward me. But boy, was Sammy popular with the girls! Maybe they liked the rebel in him. Maybe they liked his muscles. I wasn't sure, but I wanted some of that attention. I didn't have the muscles, but I decided I could start acting like a tough guy.

I recall strutting around school in the seventh grade like I was somebody to be reckoned with. I didn't physically bully anyone, but I talked tough and tried to let it be known that I wasn't someone to be messed with. As I think back, I can only imagine how strange it must've been to see such a small boy acting like a physical giant. I really did believe that acting this way would earn me respect and admiration. I desperately wanted to be liked by everyone, and I was willing to act in whatever way I needed to in order to gain acceptance, often morphing like a chameleon to be the type of person I thought others wanted me to be. I've always hated the feeling of knowing that someone else was mad at me or didn't like me. I know that need goes back to my wound of feeling unlovable as a child.

One day while in band class, I got a hall pass to go to the boy's room. While in the boy's room, another boy—a much bigger boy—came in. He was probably a foot taller than I was, and lanky with short blond hair. I recognized him as being from "The Home." The Home was what most everyone in my town called the Presbyterian Home for Children. This was a group home for kids who had been taken away from their families and sent to live in a place where they'd be raised until the State deemed it was safe for them to go back to their homes, if ever. Most of these kids had gone through much worse events in life than I had, and as a result, many of them had behavioral problems and were more likely to get into trouble at school.

Anyway, this kid came into the bathroom, grabbed me by the front of my shirt, and pinned me up against the wall. In those days we called it getting "jacked up." I'm pretty sure my feet were off the ground as I was pinned there against the cold ceramic-tile wall. He had a scowl on his face that made it look like he wanted to beat my face in. He asked me if I was scared, which in hindsight was a dumb question based on the look on my face and the tears welling up in my eyes. I sheepishly replied, "Yes."

I don't recall much else from the confrontation, other than him making me call him "sir" and "preacher," for some reason. I think once he saw that he had full control over me like a puppet for a couple of minutes, he got bored, let go of me, and left the bathroom. As soon as the coast was clear, I bolted out of there and headed back to my classroom, crying much harder now. The "tough guy" I'd been playing had been shown the door, and I was back to the realization that I was still just a weak, frightened boy.

When I got back to my classroom, my teacher asked what had happened. They found the boy, and he was punished (we received paddlings with a wooden board back then) and suspended for his actions. Thankfully, I didn't have to confront him. In fact, I never recall seeing him again.

LESSON

I'm a believer in the idea that if you don't humble yourself, life will often do it for you. I'd been strutting around school acting like a tough guy—something I wasn't. I was simply wearing a mask, a false identity, that I thought those around me would like.

We all wear masks at times. Wearing a mask might fool people for a while, but eventually your true character will be revealed (hopefully without you getting jacked up against a wall by a bully, but hey, if that's what it takes!). A few good friends later revealed to me at a church youth retreat that they actually hadn't liked the "tough guy" I'd been pretending to be. They saw past the mask I'd been wearing and told me they actually liked the regular old me just fine. But, when you grow up feeling like you're not enough, it's hard to believe otherwise overnight.

Psychoanalysis uses the term "false self" to describe behavior like mine at that time. It's a defense mechanism I used because I was unhappy with my real self. If I wasn't happy with my real self, then how is anybody else going to be? If I couldn't respect myself, how could they? I thought they couldn't. So, I only showed everyone the false self (the mask) I'd created, because I thought it'd be more respected than the real me.

When I was younger, I hated the bully that did this to me. His actions were mean and yes, they were cruel. But as I've aged and gotten smarter, I look back and feel sorry for that boy. I can only imagine what horrible things he'd been through in his life that landed him at The Home, and what wounds he was carrying as a result. Perhaps he was wearing a "tough guy" mask, as well. I'm sure that him mistreating me was a way of trying to medicate the wounds he had. I can't help but wonder if he treated me similarly to how he'd been treated in his young life. I hope he's well, wherever he is.

This bully actually did me a favor. He shattered the mask I'd been wearing. That didn't mean I wouldn't put on another mask at other times in my life, but I now had one fewer mask to choose from. It may take time, healing, or something else, but eventually you need to accept who you are and be willing to just be you. Those that accept you for you are your true friends, and the opinions of those who aren't your friends shouldn't matter to you.

TEAM APPLICATION

I've told teams I work with of my belief that respect is a foundational requirement of an effective team. Just as a home builder would first build a strong foundation before starting to build vertical walls, a team needs to build a strong foundation of respect before it can start building other necessities, like empathy and trust. If two teammates don't respect each other, how can they ever build a trusting relationship? It starts with respect.

I also believe that as important as it is that one teammate respect another, teammates have to first respect themselves. If a student-athlete lacks self-respect, they're going to have a hard time playing with confidence and having meaningful relationships with their teammates. They won't be a teammate who can be counted on to any large degree to help lead the team. I know, because I've been such a teammate.

Principle:
No one's respect is as important as my own.

CHAPTER 8

GAS STATION

Martha always encouraged Sammy and I to work. Maybe she wanted to teach us the importance of hard work and having to earn money before you could have what you wanted. Maybe she wanted to alleviate some of the financial burden of being a single guardian to two growing boys. Maybe it was a bit of both. Either way, I'm glad she did, as I believe the lessons I learned from working were a great teacher for me.

As I grew up, I remember picking up rocks in a neighbor's yard and earning a penny per rock. I remember climbing trees, picking mistletoe, and selling it door to door at Christmastime. I remember cutting a lot of lawns all around town when I got old enough to push a mower. But, my first "real" job came when I was fourteen. Martha had a friend who owned a gas station in town, and he was looking for help. I'm pretty sure it wasn't legal for me to be working at such a place at that age, but I was excited to try. I remember getting Sammy to show me how to check a car's engine oil before I went to apply for the job, just in case the boss asked me if I knew how.

Luckily, I didn't have to demonstrate any skills, and I landed the job—probably as a favor to Martha. I started working right away, mostly on weekends until the summer rolled around. I had a couple of buddies from school who also worked there, which helped make it more fun. My role started out as simply pumping gas for customers, washing windshields, and checking oil levels. Over time, I learned to add oil, change oil, and also how to fix flats and change tires. My boss was a soft-spoken, nice man whom my Aunt Martha, and many people around town really, loved and respected. He was patient to teach me how to do more around the station. Working at this job actually helped me gain confidence as I learned to take on more and more responsibilities.

And then, it started to happen.

One night I was scheduled to work until close, which was 10:30 p.m., I believe. Business was much slower that time of night, so only my boss and I were there. As we stood behind the counter, he pulled out a *Playboy* magazine and offered to let me look at the pages with him. Regrettably, this was not the first such magazine I'd seen, and although I thought it strange that a grown man was allowing me to look at it, I didn't turn down his offer. After a few minutes of perusing the pages, he reached down and pinched me in a place where a grown man shouldn't. I pulled away from him and tried my best to laugh it off, but also let him know not to do that again.

That night shook me. I didn't tell Martha. I didn't want to make it a big deal and get him in trouble—such a respected man in the community—or lose my job. I just tried to forget it. But, my boss wouldn't let me. He would pinch me repeatedly over the months I worked there, if a good opportunity presented itself. Sometimes it was on the butt, sometimes in the front. I discovered through secret conversations with my friends who also worked there that our boss did this to all of the young boys he'd hired to work for him. One boy even mentioned watching a pornographic film with our boss in the back room of the station late one night.

We all talked about how it bothered us and how wrong it was, yet none of us ever told anybody in authority who would have made it stop. Even after I left to work elsewhere, I still never told anyone. Part of me was embarrassed for allowing it to happen for so long. Part of me wanted to protect his image, for some reason. Martha spoke so highly of him, and I hated the idea of saying something that would hurt their relationship.

This man died a number of years ago. I assume his secret died with him. I omit his name on purpose, as I feel it would do no good to "out" him now. I'll let people remember him as they'd like.

LESSON

What this man did to us was wrong. My friends and I didn't ask for it, didn't want it, and we didn't deserve it. Our boss took advantage of us because of the power he had over us.

My biggest regret in this is that I apparently didn't give him a strong enough signal after the first pinch to keep him from ever touching me again. I wish I would've jumped back and loudly yelled at him, "Don't ever do that again!" I'd like to think such an action might have prevented it from ever reoccurring. But, maybe the only way to stop him would have been to quit and walk out the door, or telling an authority figure.

At my current age, it's easy for me to know now what I should have done. It's also easy for me to imagine how I would react if that happened to me now, being a full-grown man. I wouldn't tolerate it. But, these situations rarely happen to full-grown men. People like this man prey upon young kids, the seemingly weak and vulnerable, those they feel they can disrespect in such a way and not get caught.

I failed to use the power of my voice (I could have told Martha or the police), and I failed to use the power of my actions (I could have quit the job and never returned). Because I didn't do either of these things, I allowed the perpetrator to maintain power over me. I've carried guilt about these incidents because of my lack of action. By doing nothing, I failed myself, the other boys employed there, and any other boys who may have worked there after I left. It sickens me to think about what else this man may have gotten away with because of my failure to speak up.

If I had spoken up, I likely would have experienced some sort of discomfort or pain. I might not have been believed, which would have hurt me emotionally. I might have been told to keep my mouth shut so as not to damage this well-respected man's reputation. This man might have even tried to get back at me in some way. There would have certainly been the discomfort of fear in speaking up. Yet, I've learned that any discomfort I would have faced would have been temporary. The regret that I live with is permanent.

TEAM APPLICATION

In sports, you may sometimes hear a coach say, "Pain is temporary" as you're grinding through a tough workout or practice. That statement is so true. One reason

I love sports so much is because it's a microcosm of what life is like. Like the temporary pain we experience when we prepare our bodies for physical competition, life outside of sports will present us with temporary pain and discomfort, as well. It may feel like it's going to last forever, but it never does. Pain never lasts forever, but both pride and regret do.

Sometimes when we suffer through the temporary pain or discomfort, we end up with such a sense of pride—that feeling of, "I can't believe I survived that!" I've had many student-athletes enjoy that feeling after completing Battle-Tested events. It helps boost their confidence in themselves and in each other.

Other times, the temporary pain and discomfort leave us with a lot of regret—regret because perhaps we gave into the pain and quit, we only gave partial effort to reduce the pain, or we avoided the pain altogether by not showing up (either physically or mentally). These experiences can damage the confidence of the student-athlete and reduce the amount of trust that teammates and coaches have in them.

The most successful student-athletes recognize that pain is temporary, realize that suffering through it benefits them, and embrace the opportunities to step into the pain.

Principle:
My pain and discomfort are temporary,
but pride and regret last forever.

Me around fourteen years old,
when I started working at the gas station

CHAPTER 9

THE BATTING HELMET

Marc Scarbrough has been one of my best friends since middle school. Marc moved to Talladega when I was in eighth grade, and we clicked instantly. I can still remember when and where we met. I think I spent the night at his house within the first week of meeting. Marc's house became a big hang-out place for our group of friends for several reasons: One, his parents were cool with it; two, he had a lot of open land around his house great for football, baseball, and basketball; and three, Marc had a hot older sister, Tammy.

We spent the majority of our time in the grass field to the side of Marc's house when the weather was good. We played many hours of football there, and it's where I built my sterling reputation as an undersized football dynamo.

One beautiful summer day, I rode my bike over to Marc's to meet up with some friends to play a game. We didn't have enough guys show up for a good game of football, so we decided to play wiffle ball. Because of the small number of friends who showed up, we would have to play "straight base," where you play with only a home plate and one base. I don't recall everyone there that day, but I certainly remember Marc and our friend Freddie Peninger.

I had met Freddie a couple years prior when his family moved to Talladega and we landed on the same Little League baseball team. Freddie and I actually share the same birthday, and we became best friends quickly. He was fun to be around, a great athlete, and was really popular with the girls. Freddie and his family became like family to me over the next few years. I spent many nights at their house, and they even invited Sammy and me on a family vacation with them one year.

Marc had a plastic bat and ball for us to play the game with, but we needed to create a home plate and the base before we could get started. Someone offered up their T-shirt for home plate. I happened to be wearing my Pittsburgh Pirates plastic batting helmet (the one my mom bought me at Six Flags). I offered it up to be used as the base, but under one condition. I told the guys clearly that it was not to be stepped on. You would be considered "safe" as long as you were standing next to the helmet.

Very early in the game, Freddie hit the ball, ran to the base where my helmet sat, and jumped straight onto it, crushing it purposefully under both feet. I was pissed. This wasn't the first time Freddie had shown disregard for either his property or mine, so in hindsight I shouldn't have been surprised, but I was ticked off at him. Perhaps Freddie thought it was just a cheap old helmet and he could probably get some laughs by crushing it. He likely thought it could be easily replaced. He was wrong. Despite my anger, we did finish the wiffle ball game, now using the crushed helmet as base.

That night after I got home and sat alone in my room, I couldn't stop thinking about that helmet. I realized that it truly was the only possession I had that had been given to me by my mom. I realized in that moment how special that helmet was to me. I began to cry. Nope, I began to sob. I sobbed over the thought of no longer having that helmet, over the thought of not having a relationship with my mom. That helmet had served as some sort of link to her—the only link I still had—and now it was gone. I was devastated.

I sheepishly went to see Martha in the family room, looking for comfort. I found it. She held me and told me how sorry she was. It's exactly what you'd expect a mother to do: console her hurting son. Martha mothered me as best she could. She'd done her best to mother Sammy and me, and provide us with the best upbringing she could. I'll always be indebted to her for her sacrifice of taking in two boys to raise as her own.

As I cried in her arms, Martha took her parenting to a different level. She called Sammy into the family room. I didn't really want Sammy to see my crying like I was, but it's likely he'd already heard me, anyway. When he came into the room, Martha said, "Sammy, I want you to walk over to Marc's house with Blake and bring every piece of that helmet home."

Wow! Unexpected. Going over the next morning would have been just fine, but Martha obviously saw how important this was to me, and that made it important to her. It was well past dark by now, so Martha gave us a flashlight, and Sammy and I walked less than a mile to Marc's house.

I don't recall what we discussed along the way, but I remember that Sammy never made fun of me or teased me about crying, which I had expected him to do. Sammy and I disagreed on a lot of things in life, and we fought a lot, but this was a mission I think we both felt was important, like we were on the search for a missing family member.

Sammy longed for our birth family to be reunited more than I did, and I think he could appreciate what that helmet meant to me. The kindness he showed me that night is probably my favorite memory of Sammy. He was the ultimate big brother to me in that moment.

Sammy and I arrived to Marc's yard, and with the help of the flashlight, picked up every piece of that helmet, placed it all in a plastic bag that Martha had given us, and walked home together. Even though it was broken into pieces, at least I would still have that link to my mom. I thought I'd probably stick the bag of helmet pieces in a drawer for safekeeping and pull it out when I wanted to feel that connection to my mom.

When Sammy and I walked through the back door into the kitchen, we found Martha seated at the kitchen table waiting for us with a bottle of super glue. The three of us spent the rest of the night piecing that helmet back together, like a Franken-helmet. I wish I could say that you could hardly notice the repairs, but you could. I would never wear the helmet out in public again, but I would be able to put it in a place of prominence in my room and be reminded of how broken things can be mended.

LESSON

In some ways, that broken helmet was a mirror of my young life: a family was shattered into pieces under the foot of a strong force against it. But, broken families are a lot harder to put back together than plastic helmets, and they require a lot more than super glue. I guess that's why most never get mended. There's just too much pain, damage, anger, and whatever else to get past. Yet, what Martha and Sammy showed me that night was that you can piece together a family out of what you have, even if it's not the most conventional.

There's a time to mourn broken families (and broken helmets), and then there's a time to pick up the pieces, put them together as best you can, and move forward. You have to work with the pieces you have left after the damage is done and make the best of the situation. I couldn't change the fact that my helmet was broken and would never be the same again. I couldn't change the fact that my family was broken and would never be the same again. But, I could change the way I looked at life and attempt to make it the best I could.

I used to look back on my young life with a lot of disappointment. I used to think, *Why did all those things have to happen to me?* I had the mentality of a victim who only saw the pain in the situation and often felt like the world owed me something because of all the crap I had to go through. My life changed when I realized this principle: **Life doesn't happen to you; it happens for you.** All the things I've gone through in life, good and bad, have been for my benefit. Yes, they were often painful and depressing, but those things helped prepare me for the work that I do now through Battle-Tested, in my family, and in my community.

TEAM APPLICATION

Every team goes through many different experiences, both good and bad, throughout their existence. They may experience the highs of great team-building or team-bonding events, winning streaks, upset wins, breaking school records, and winning a championship. They may also experience the lows of injury, upset losses, division among teammates, loss of a teammate, poor grades, bullying, lack of playing time, and failing to reach team goals. All of these things are events. Events happen to us all the time that we have little or no control over.

What we do have control over is the way we respond to the events. The way we respond to an event will affect the outcome of the event. The better our responses, the better the outcomes.

For example, if I make an error in the field (event) and I get angry at myself, kick the dirt, and lose it mentally (response), I'm more likely to make another error or get pulled from the game by my coach (outcome). In the same example, if I make an error in the field (event), and I yell out to my teammates, "My bad! I'll get the next one!" and show confidence in my body language (response), I'm much more likely to make the play next time and get to remain in the game (outcome).

There's an equation for what I'm describing here: Event + Response = Outcome (E + R = O). Teammates who have the best responses to the events that they face will have the best outcomes. Simple to say and understand, much harder to do.

Principle:
The better my response, the better the outcome.

My Franken-helmet

CHAPTER 10

OLYMPIC DREAMS

I've always loved watching the Olympics, especially the Summer Olympics. I've always been drawn to the track-and-field events. In the summer of 1984, the Summer Games were in Los Angeles, and I watched them daily. Carl Lewis of the US dominated, winning four gold medals. I was inspired! I fell in love with the long jump. I loved to jump (what boy doesn't?), and it sure looked like a whole lot of fun to defy gravity and land in a sand pit.

After watching the long-jump event on TV, I vividly remember telling Sammy I was going to be in the Olympics someday. I walked out the back door, hopped on my bike, and rode to the track-and-field facility at the Alabama School for the Deaf, located a couple of miles from my house. I had all the confidence in the world that I could make it happen!

This was the only long jump pit I knew of in Talladega, and I just knew this would be where the road to Olympic glory would begin for me. The track was empty on that hot, humid summer day. It was clear that I was going to be the only one from Talladega to make it to the Olympics, since nobody else was there putting in work.

I began practicing, trying my best to imitate what I'd

just seen Carl Lewis do. I knew the road to the Olympics would be a long one, but I was gaining confidence with each jump I made.

After a few jumps into my practice session, I saw Sammy and one of our neighborhood friends, Mike, riding their bikes down Cherry Street alongside the track. Mike was three years older than me. He was a great guy I really looked up to, a terrific athlete, and definitely one of the cool kids. As they rode past the track I heard Mike yell, "Boy! You ain't going to the Olympics!" Those were his exact words. They're engrained in my memory as if chiseled in stone. I stared at Mike and Sammy until they were out of sight, my mind beginning to process what I'd just heard.

Was Mike right? Was this just a stupid dream that had no chance of coming true? Was I just wasting my time out there all alone in the heat? All these questions flooded my mind, and they linked arms with the "I am not enough" voice already present in my brain.

I walked down the track and through the gate, got on my bike, and defeatedly rode home. As quickly as the dream had came to be, I quit on it just as fast.

LESSON

I already struggled to find belief in my abilities to succeed in life, and Mike's words acted as a reminder for me that I didn't have what it takes. My dream was dashed before it ever really had a chance to bloom. Man, I wish I could have been there on that track to speak to fourteen-year-old Blake. I could have encouraged him in the pursuit of his dreams. I could have been a Jimbo for him. There were plenty of naysayers to go around, including himself, but if just one person would have been there to say, "If you work long enough and hard enough, it just might be possible," maybe he would have continued to put in work in that pit, and hey, who knows? Maybe Olympic gold. Maybe a college scholarship. Maybe increased confidence and success. Maybe a greater work ethic is developed.

So many good things might have come from ignoring the doubt and embracing the pit— embracing the fact that it's going to take a lot of hard work to accomplish any big dream in life. If we're going to quit on a dream the minute one person doubts us, we shouldn't dream at all. Is it risky to pursue your dreams? Heck yeah! But, it's your choice: are you going to be a risk taker or a dream waster? If you're not willing to pursue your dreams, then leave the dreaming to someone else. Give your dreams to someone who'll actually do something with them.

TEAM APPLICATION

All students should have dreams. They may dream about getting into a certain college or of a certain career. Many student-athletes have dreams about their sport (i.e. winning seasons, championships, etc.). High school athletes might dream of playing in college or even earning a college scholarship. College players might dream of national championships, playing professionally, or getting into coaching. I work with a lot of athletes who don't have dreams of athletics beyond their current level, and that's okay, too. But, we should all have dreams that we're chasing.

Dreams are like newborn babies in that they're so dependent on others to take good care of them, nurture them, and love them so they can grow to reach their full potential. In order for a dream to have a chance of becoming reality, the dream must be paired with someone who will give it the attention and effort it needs. Is that you? What dreams do you have? Are you taking risks to make those dreams come true, or are your dreams wasting away?

Principle:
I will be a dream chaser.

CHAPTER 11

FOOTBALL

During my junior year of high school, a couple of my friends thought it would be a great idea for our circle of friends to all join the football team. Most of us had never played football before, or maybe a year of peewee league, which was my experience. We played a ton of backyard football at my friend Marc's house. I felt like I was a pretty good backyard football player—small, but quick—so making the transition to high school football shouldn't have been that difficult, so I thought.

I also felt that being on the football team would help me become more popular. Maybe there was a special power in the red Talladega High School Tigers jersey, because wearing them seemed to make you instantly popular and cool—something I definitely felt I needed help with in high school. The players wore their jerseys to school on game-day Fridays. There was a pep rally every game day, where the players would all be loudly celebrated by the entire school. Who wouldn't want that? I sure did!

On a hot first day of football practice, the coaches had me practice at receiver. Excellent decision on their part, I thought! This was one of my specialties in backyard football, and I felt like I really practiced well at receiver that day. First day of practice for my friend Chris Cotter didn't go so well. Chris was the only one in our circle of friends shorter than me at the time (just barely). He was holding a blocking dummy in a drill on the first day when a player hit it, breaking Chris's thumb so bad that he had to have surgery to repair it. Who knew holding a blocking dummy could be so dangerous? Maybe the injury was a result of poor coaching. Regardless, day one, Chris's high school football career was over.

On day two, the coaches switched me over to the defensive side of the ball. What? I had just showed them the previous day my amazing receiving skills! I couldn't believe their decision. I was upset, but in hindsight they likely just wanted to see where I fit best by trying me in different positions.

On the first drill of the practice, they lined me up at defensive back, the position that defends the wide receivers. They put me in front of a line with other defensive backs and told us all, "You and a running back are going to run and meet at the sideline. Your job is to knock the running back out of bounds." I thought that sounded simple enough. That was, until I looked across the field to see the running back that I was to be knocking out of bounds. It was "Rock." Rock and I had been friends since third grade (he may have even been on the playground during the chipmunk incident). He earned the nickname Rock because he was built like one. He had muscles on top of his muscles. He was our team's starting tailback. He was the same age as me, but he went through puberty well before I did.

The whistle blew, and Rock and I raced toward destiny at the sideline. When we got there, Rock lowered his shoulder into me, resulting in a loud clap of pads colliding.

He absolutely ran me over! I slowly peeled myself up off the grass and stepped off the field next to the sideline where I'd just been buried. It quickly became apparent to me that I could no longer feel or move my right arm.

A trainer met me there on the sideline. The thunderous sound of getting my world rocked probably signaled him over. When I told him of my ailment, he replied, "Ah. That's just a stinger, Blake! The feeling will come back in about ten minutes, and when it does, you let me know and I'll send you back out there."

Ten minutes came and went . . . twenty minutes . . . a half hour . . . an hour. Oh sure, the feeling did come back in about ten minutes, but there was no way I was going to tell the trainer that. There was no way I was going to go back out there and risk getting hit like that again. I remained on the sidelines, too afraid to try again. On day two of tryouts, one hit from Rock ended my football career.

LESSON

I actually don't blame Rock for ending my football career; I blame myself. It was my decision. I allowed my fear and self-doubt to prevent me from playing the game. I let my fear steal my lunch money. You see, that one hit confirmed for me what I already believed about myself: *I don't have what it takes to play high school football.* Because of the small size of my body and the negative voice in my head, I already felt like I wasn't "man enough" to play for the Talladega Tigers. I was hoping to prove that I could, and step into being more of a man, but apparently I wasn't ready to make that jump yet.

I'm guessing that at some point in your life, you've

failed at something, taken a blow to your ego, got hit so hard that you had to slump away to recover from your wound. You've retreated to the sideline, no longer willing or wanting to get back into the game. You've believed the game was too big for you, that you weren't able to play the game at the required level, or that the game was meant for others, but not for you.

If you're not careful, you'll allow yourself to remain on that sideline and let life pass you by. Sure, it's safe on the sideline. You can't get hurt on the sideline. But, there's no real life on the sideline. There's no joy there: it's hollow, lonely, and full of regret. Victories don't happen on the sideline.

When we receive that devastating hit, we've got to insert ourselves back onto the field as quickly as possible. The longer we remain on the sideline, the harder it is to leave its comfort. Getting back on the field is risky and can be extremely frightening, but I've learned that failing on the field is better than fearing on the sideline. Said another way, a life with little risk enjoys little reward. Sure, failure can hurt, but it doesn't hurt as much as the sour taste of regret you have to live with because you were too afraid to try.

TEAM APPLICATION

Sports offer us up so many opportunities to fail, and yet we still choose to participate. Some failures on the field are much bigger than others. We see athletes fail to come through at the end of the game, and their team winds up losing. Even though the team could have done more earlier in the game to put the game out of reach, it's the failure at the end of the game that's remembered.

I realize my football story doesn't apply to all student-athletes, especially at the collegiate level. There are some student-athletes with plenty of confidence in their abilities who bounce back from failures extremely well. There are also some who have a strong desire to be in the high-pressure situation when the game is on the line. Even so, I also know that I'm not alone.

There may be athletes on your team who have a huge fear of failure. They hope their number isn't called when the game is close and it would be up to them to win the game. Maybe they've assigned too much of their self-worth to their success in their sport, and they believe that it would just crush them to let down the team. They likely think their coaches, teammates, and parents would be so disappointed in them if they failed.

In order to combat this fear, coaches and teammates need to celebrate not just those who come through in the clutch, but also those who are willing to try, even if they fail. Teammates need to learn to accept that yes, at times they will fail in their sport, but victory can be found in giving their best effort and in being willing to throw their hat in the ring. No defeat lessens their value as a person.

Principle:
I will choose to fail on the field rather than fear on the sideline.

CHAPTER 12

TRACK SEASON

After my big fail on the football field in the fall of my junior year and licking my wounds through the winter, I was looking for some redemption the following spring. I also wanted another opportunity to get my picture in the yearbook. I decided to join the track team.

The best part of joining the track team was that there were no tryouts. If you simply showed up to the first meeting, you were on the team. Easy enough! And guess what? They took the team photo for the yearbook at that first meeting. My true mission was accomplished then and there! Anything else the season held in store was really inconsequential. The yearbook would be lasting evidence that I was a card-carrying member of the track team that year.

Now, to be honest, a part of me thought that being on the track team would not be very physically demanding. After all, it wasn't a contact sport where someone like Rock would be able to destroy me with one vicious hit. I used to jog around the neighborhood a good bit, and I even owned a jogging suit, so I had that going for me. Well, it turned out, the coach actually wanted us to run much faster than a jog, and for much longer distances than

I normally ran. I soon realized I was going to challenged much more than I had hoped.

Talladega High School did not have its own track. We practiced and had our home meets at the Alabama School for the Deaf, the same place where my Olympic dreams had been crushed a couple years prior. My skill set, or lack thereof, landed me in one field event and two track events that season. I competed in the high jump, which was inappropriately named, in my case. There were plenty others on the team with better "hops" than me, but I was able to demonstrate good form—known as the "Fosbury flop" — so I was chosen to compete. Despite my lack of talent in the high jump, I did enjoy it. I liked that it was not a strenuous event, and I liked the challenge of trying to get up and over that bar.

The two track events I was placed in were what really soured my track-team experience. I had dreams of replicating Carl Lewis and running the 100M, but despite my speed on the backyard football field, it turned out I was a lot slower than the athletes on the team who had actually hit puberty, while I was still looking for my first armpit hair in the mirror every night. I was assigned to the 800M and the two-mile relay, which meant I had to run 800M in two different events.

If you're not familiar with the 800M, it's running (or trying to run) twice around the track at near full-sprinting speed. Miserable! Outside of Olympians, I'm not sure who could do that, but it wasn't this guy. I could jog the first lap and a half, and give out a little sprint in the last straightaway. I hated this race. If you really pushed yourself the way you were expected to, there was a good chance you'd vomit soon thereafter. And hey, I was just here to get my picture taken for the yearbook, remember?

I no longer had Olympic dreams, especially if those dreams included running until I puked.

It's a bit embarrassing to tell the story, but I vividly recall running a halfhearted two-mile relay with my teammates, knowing that a little later I'd be asked to run the 800M individual event. Before the runners were called to the starting line for the 800M, I ran (not fast) and hid behind a big green dumpster just behind the stadium seating. When someone came looking for me, I pretended to be puking from the previous race.

Unlike the fear that I experienced in my high school football story, my reason for hiding behind the dumpster was based more on a lack of desire than a lack of courage. Yes, I felt a little bad about my decision to hide behind the dumpster, but I was happy I got out of running the race.

LESSON

This story clearly describes one major principle I've learned through this experience and others like it. This principle has proven to be one of the biggest truths I've learned in life: the size of your "why" dictates the size of your work. If you have a strong reason ("why") for doing something (i.e. participating in a sport, being named all-conference, losing weight, getting into that certain college, etc.), you will put in greater effort than if you care very little about that thing.

My "why" for being on the track team was very small (picture in the yearbook), so I gave little effort to becoming the best track athlete I could. I had an 8:00 a.m. aerobics class one semester in college that I really didn't want to be a part of. I hated getting up early, and at the time, I thought aerobics was really just for women. I found it pretty easy to sleep in and skip a few too many classes, which caused my grade to suffer. Had I really wanted to be an aerobics instructor, or really needed to get in shape, or wanted to spend time with a really cute girl in the class, I likely would've showed up, participated in every class, and earned an A in the class.

TEAM APPLICATION

I'm guessing that you can think of similar examples in your life. Memories of these moments can sometimes generate regret over our lack of dedication to something or someone that deserved better from us. The bottom line is that before we make a commitment (to a team, employer, or person), we need to make sure our "why" is large enough to motivate us to give our best. If we don't have a strong "why," then everyone is likely better off if we save our commitments for another time.

As a student-athlete, it's best if your motivation comes from within (intrinsic motivation). If you're motivated to play a sport because others want you to (extrinsic motivation), then when things get challenging, your "why" may not be big enough to motivate you to continually give the team your all through the hard times. I see this in high school sports commonly. A student-athlete joins a team because their best friend is on the team, or simply to stay in shape, or because they feel pressure from their parents. These athletes can lack motivation to give it their all when workouts and practices get tough and seasons grow long. On the other hand, when I see a high school athlete playing because they know that a college scholarship in a sport is their only way to go to college (and they dream of going to college), I see tremendous work ethic.

You need to discover your "why," and if you feel it's not big enough to push you to give your team your best, you need to consider not being on the team, or see if you can find a bigger "why." Great success in any area of life requires great sacrifice and perhaps great pain. You likely will not sacrifice greatly or endure great pain unless you have a strong "why' for achieving success.

Principle:
The size of my "why" dictates the size of my work.

CHAPTER 13

STINKY FEET

Attending youth group at the First United Methodist Church was a big part of my high school years. We met on Sunday and Wednesday nights, and it was usually pretty well attended. Adult leaders came and went with some frequency, but I always seemed to enjoy whoever was in charge at the moment. Being a part of the youth group helped fulfill my basic human need to be a part of a group. We went on fun retreats regularly and served in the community, which helped teach me the value of serving others.

On one particular Sunday night, I showed up to youth group and learned that we would be washing each other's feet. This is not an uncommon practice in the Christian church, as Jesus modeled it for us when he washed his disciples' feet. I knew it was meant to be a serious and reflective time—a religious ceremony of sorts—that was to be treated with reverence. I also knew that my feet smelled really bad.

Although I didn't grow up in poverty, I did live in a single-income family (Martha was an educator at the Alabama School for the Deaf), and new clothes and shoes weren't high on the priority list. I wore lots of Sammy's hand-me-downs, which were usually hand-me-downs from some other family in town that had given clothes to Martha for Sammy and me. I usually had to wear the same pair of shoes for a long period of time. I recall, on more than one occasion, sitting in school, smelling a foul odor, and wondering who smelled so bad. Only later did I realize that it was the smell of my stinky shoes rising up from under my desk. Super embarrassing!

That night at youth group, I hid under the pool table on the opposite side of the room while others assembled in a circle of folding chairs. I didn't want anyone to be anywhere close to my stinky feet. I watched from floor level as one by one, students knelt down in front of someone of their choice with a bedpan filled with water and a washrag.

After a few minutes, people realized I was missing from the circle, and I was discovered in my hiding spot. It took a lot of coercion, but I finally came out from under the pool table and joined the others in the circle. I was so uncomfortable!

After a few minutes, one of my classmates came and kneeled down in front of me with the bedpan and washrag. This was quickly becoming one of my worst nightmares, not just because of what was about to happen, but because of who kneeled down in front of me. It was Susan! Yes, the same Susan from the third-grade chipmunk incident. Are you kidding me? Susan and I never dated, but were great friends. I cared greatly about what she thought of me. I just knew she would never see me the same once she got a whiff of my feet. Any hopes of a future prom date with her were about to be dashed!

The situation was growing into something I didn't think I could handle. In that moment, which was supposed to be reverent and solemn, I decided to pick up my bare feet and quickly slam them down into the bedpan, splashing water and foot funk all over Susan as I laughed out loud. Nobody else joined me in my laughter, especially not Susan. As she kneeled there at my feet, partially soaked with water, she looked up at me with her big hazel eyes. Susan had looked at me lots of different ways throughout the years of our friendship, but this look was one I'd never seen before and never wanted to see again. It was a look of sadness and disappointment. It only took that one look from Susan to cut through all the self-centered emotions I'd been feeling. I felt horrible, and was filled with regret for my stupid, immature reaction to the situation.

I can't recall if I verbally said I was sorry in that moment—I sure hope I did—but I do remember what happened next. Susan could have stood and moved on to someone else in the circle who would appreciate her humble gesture. I certainly deserved that (and worse), and I probably would have been more comfortable if that had been her choice. Instead, she picked up the washrag and proceeded to wash my feet with what little water was left in the bedpan. Then, she took the time to dry both feet.

Susan didn't give me what I deserved. She gave me what I needed: mercy.

LESSON

When I faced adversity in this story (the discomfort of having to allow someone else to wash my stinky feet), I handled it poorly. At first I hid, trying to avoid the uncomfortable situation, which perhaps has been the most favorite self-defense tactic I've used throughout my life. And then, when I couldn't avoid the discomfort, I tried to use my second favorite self-defense tactic—humor—to reduce the tension myself and others might've felt in the uncomfortable moment.

On the contrary, when Susan faced adversity in this story (the disrespect I showed her and the now-soggy clothes she wore), she handled it with poise, grace, and forgiveness. She didn't let the adversity stop her from doing what she set out to do. She certainly could have thrown in the towel and screamed, "I didn't sign up for this!" Instead, Susan provided a great example of how to handle adversity we face in life. I'm convinced that the people in this world who achieve the most success in life have found a way to handle adversity better than others. They don't let rejection, failure, or any adversity stop them from moving forward. They don't let fear and discomfort affect their commitment levels. They abandon their excuses. These words don't always describe me, but I'm continually trying to improve so that they will one day.

Around the age of thirty, Susan had a series of strokes that nearly took her life and left her bound to a wheelchair. Her vision and speech are impaired, as well as the use of her arms. Many would have thrown in the towel when faced with this adversity, but once again, Susan found a way to handle it and have a successful life, regardless of her circumstances.

TEAM APPLICATION

The adversities we face in life always provide us with opportunities. Our challenge is to see the opportunities in the adversity and try to make the most of them. Adversity provides opportunities for growth.

- Does one of your teammates rub you the wrong way?
- Is your team filled with negative attitudes?
- Have you been disrespected by a teammate and need to have an uncomfortable conversation to address it?
- Has your coach asked you to play a position you're not comfortable with?
- Has a valued member of your team been lost to injury?
- Have you had a significant injury?
- Have you lost playing time to an underclassman?
- Has your team lost a game it had no business losing?

All of these adversities present growth opportunities. Since we can't avoid adversity in life, we should make every effort to learn from those situations to make us better going forward. Having this type of mindset will not only make it easier to tolerate adversity, it will also make you more successful as a team.

Principle:
I find opportunity in adversity.

CHAPTER 14

BETRAYAL

The fall of 1987 brought about my senior year of high school. I was looking forward to being the "big man on campus" despite not having fully realized puberty yet. However, instead of it being one of the best years ever, it held in store for me one of the worst times of my life.

I never had a steady girlfriend in high school. I went on a few dates, but those were mostly to the dances held by the school or Double Nine (a sorority in our high school). I did have strong interest in a few girls, but they never seemed to show the same level of interest in me.

My best friend, Marc, was a junior that year and had a girlfriend who was a freshman in college. Because I hung out at Marc's house all the time, the three of us had spent a lot of time together the previous summer. I was okay with playing the third wheel, because I didn't have much else to do, anyway, and because Marc was my best friend. When she came to town to visit during her fall semester of college, the three of us hung out then, too.

Christmas break finally arrived, and the three of us once again were together all the time. We'd been riding around town drinking a few beers when Marc said he needed to be dropped off at home because his family was leaving for Opelika, Alabama, to visit relatives. For some reason, I stayed with his girlfriend. We drove to the grade school that I had attended through second grade. The old Central School had closed long before, but had been bought by the First Baptist Church next door and was mostly used as a hangout for youth events. It was empty that day, but she had a key because of the position her dad held in the church. It was empty except for us.

We watched TV on a couch in one of the former class-rooms, and she asked if she could scratch my back. I said, "Sure." Before I knew it, we were kissing. Unfortunately, my first thought afterward was not about Marc, but about me. I thought about how great it was to have a girl inter-ested in me. To be honest, I hadn't really seen this girl in a romantic way before, but now I was seeing her in a differ-ent light. I wasn't used to having a girl pursue me, and it felt really good. It was validating for me, something I longed for in my life. I fell hook, line, and sinker.

I wish I could say it ended there, but it didn't. She and I carried on an affair behind Marc's back for close to two months. When she went back to college, we spoke on the phone a lot. I even took a weekend trip to her college to visit her, telling Marc I was going there to go on a date with one of her friends. The deceit was horrible, and it's painful to relive the story here.

One weekend, she came back to town to visit, and once again the three of us were out together. She had been tell-ing me she was going to break up with Marc so that she and I could be together. I believed her, and I thought that's what I wanted, as well. We stopped to use the restroom at a fast-food restaurant while Marc stayed in the car.

When we got back to the car, we found him in tears, demanding we take him home. He had found her phone bill while we were inside the restaurant, and had seen all the phone calls she'd made to my home number. He now knew about us. I was so blinded with ignorance, and what I thought was love, that I selfishly thought that now, finally, she and I would get to be together. We didn't. She chose to try to reconcile with Marc instead of pursuing a relationship with me.

I was devastated. I had just lost my best friend and the girl I thought I loved. Marc was devastated. He had just lost his best friend and his girlfriend. It was all an absolutely painful mess. I deserved what I got. Marc didn't.

For what felt like weeks, I didn't smile, and I seldom spoke at school. There was nothing to smile about. I was filled with shame and regret. Marc ended his relationship with the girl. I apologized profusely to Marc for what I'd done and the pain I'd caused him. He forgave me enough to where we could be civil with each other, but the rest of my senior year went by without being able to claim things were back to normal or that we were still best friends.

Marc and I lost our close contact during our college years. I do recall feeling the need to apologize to him over and over again whenever I'd see him. I just never felt like words could express how sorry I was. The good news is that Marc did indeed forgive me, and still loved me, and he still does to this day. Marc is once again one of my best friends. We've done a number of golf trips together, and I stop to see him when I visit Alabama, where I know I always have a place to stay.

LESSON

Forgiveness can be such a hard concept to fully learn. As painful as it was, Marc has shown me what true forgiveness looks and feels like. I certainly didn't feel like I was worthy of his forgiveness. Would I have been able to forgive like that if the shoe had been on the other foot? I like to think so, but I'm not sure.

I heard a quote once that said something along the lines of, "Those who have been greatly forgiven find it easier to forgive others." I certainly know that Marc forgave me for a great transgression I committed against him. Before I ever became a Christian, Marc was giving me a glimpse of what it looked and felt like to be forgiven by God.

Marc forgave me long before I was willing to accept his forgiveness. Because I felt so unworthy of his forgiveness, I felt like it shouldn't be given to me so easily. Surely I should have to serve out some form of punishment first. Surely I have to work to make amends in some way. Marc didn't demand that of me.

Throughout my life, I've always found it easier to forgive others than to forgive myself. It's as if I feel others are worthy of being forgiven, but I'm not. I'm much harder on myself for my mistakes than I am on others for theirs. The truth is, if I'm truly sorry for my mistakes, I am worthy of forgiveness . . . and so are you.

TEAM APPLICATION

Teammates and coaches will wrong each other. Usually it's not intentional, but because we're human, we will make mistakes that hurt each other. We might disrespect someone, deceive someone, or we might even do something dumb like I did to Marc. When these things happen, there is the potential for team relations to break down so that the team no longer functions well. I hear about it happening more than I'd like. As a team, we need to be willing to forgive each other and ourselves.

Both asking for and granting forgiveness require humility. The one who needs to be forgiven must be able to humble themselves in order to see how their words or actions have hurt a teammate. They must also have humility to genuinely want to make things right and seek forgiveness. The one who needs to forgive a teammate also needs to humble themselves to remove any pride that would prevent them from granting forgiveness to someone asking for it.

I didn't learn this until I got older, but when we forgive others, it sets us free. Forgiving others frees us from any anger or resentment we might be feeling toward a teammate. It allows us to be more positive. The more positive we are, the more likely we are to be successful in our sport, and of course we'll be a better teammate, as well. Forgiving ourselves is also very freeing, and helps us be our best self for our team.

We all make mistakes. Maybe you've made a big one, but that doesn't mean you aren't worthy of forgiveness.

Principle:
I am worthy of forgiveness, and so are my teammates.

Marc and me on a boat trip during a golf trip
to Gulf Shores, Alabama, in 2010

CHAPTER 15

SALVATION

In the summer of 1989, I was back in Talladega after completing a successful freshman year at the University of Montevallo. I did well in my classes, made some great friends, and had started dating a girl when the school year had started the previous August.

My girlfriend was a year older, and we'd met the previous summer through a mutual friend. She was from Lincoln, Alabama, which is just a few miles north of Talladega. She had the most amazing parents! That's one thing I looked for in a girlfriend, actually. I wanted to date someone whose parents were still married. I hoped to one day marry into a family that represented what the ideal family should look like to me—not like the one I came from.

Her dad was a minister of a small Methodist church in their hometown. He was extremely well respected and a very funny and engaging man. Her mom was perhaps one of the sweetest, most loving women I've ever met, and always greeted me with a big hug. We drove from Montevallo to visit them most every weekend while we were dating, so I spent a lot of time at their house during my freshman year. They always made me feel so welcomed and loved. I would often attend church with them when I was home on the weekends.

On June 1, 1989, my girlfriend and I made plans to spend the day together. That afternoon, we went to watch a softball game nearby that some friends of mine were playing in. I don't recall a thing about the game, but I do remember who else was there. It was Marc's ex-girlfriend whom I wrote about earlier. I hadn't seen or heard from her since the big ordeal that had gone down between her, Marc, and me. Needless to say, I was more than a little uncomfortable to see her and to later have to explain to my girlfriend who this girl was as we drove back to her parent's house.

She was disappointed to hear the story, and I was more disappointed to tell it. As we reached the driveway of her parent's house, I was overcome with emotion. I started crying uncontrollably. I didn't really know why initially as my girlfriend questioned me, "What's wrong?" I composed myself enough to say, "I want to become a Christian." To which she replied, "What? I thought you already were."

Up until that point, I would have called myself a Christian if anyone had asked. Sammy and I had gone through some sort of confirmation-type thing in the Methodist church we grew up in. I believe I was thirteen at the time. I didn't remember much about it, just that Martha made us do it and that I got water sprinkled on my head during church one morning. I also had gone down front during an altar call in a citywide revival when I was in eighth grade, but that was because the cute girl sitting next to me did.

When my girlfriend and I had first started dating, she asked me to stop drinking and swearing. I attended church with her pretty regularly. By all outward appearances, most people probably would've assumed I was a Christian. But, in that driveway on June 1, 1989, it became very clear to me that I wasn't. I was flooded with guilt and shame for the sins I'd committed in my life, and I knew I needed forgiveness.

We went inside her parent's house. Her mom was home, and right then and there her mom led me in a prayer of salvation. I'll never forget that day and the new sense of faith, hope, and excitement I had. I started reading the Bible and praying daily, and when I arrived back at Montevallo that fall, I joined the Campus Outreach ministry. It was there that I'd learn so much more about how to grow as a Christian.

I fully believe that God puts people in our lives for a season with specific purposes in mind. Though my relationship with that girlfriend ended the following December, I am so thankful that God used her and her amazing family to draw me to Him. I heard her parents both died years ago. I sure hope to see them in Heaven one day!

LESSON

I see my salvation on June 1, 1989, as a second birthday. I was going to turn nineteen on June 5, but I felt like I was just coming to life. I had a new sense of hope. It felt like I had a lot of weight that I had been carrying taken off my shoulders. I felt like I'd gained a father that day—a father who would not leave me, but would always be present for me, look after me, and would help father me in ways that I needed.

I know some good people in this world who claim no

faith and no belief in the God of the Bible, or any god, for that matter. I just don't see how they do it. I know that faith comes easier for some people than others, but for me, I can look back at the story of my life and see what I believe to be the hand of God with me all along. Even before I fully believed in Him, He was looking after me. Even when I cursed His name, He cared for me.

When I was young and believed that my family had given me away, I used to think that I had been "set aside." Now, I know that I'd been "set apart" to do some very special work that God has been equipping me to accomplish.

TEAM APPLICATION

I have a strong belief in God and the role that He has played, and will play, in my life. That belief has made me a better person. My belief in God has helped me to develop a greater belief in myself and others around me. I think I would feel lost without this belief I have.

Teammates need to have belief in the team and belief in each other. Coaches need to have belief in their players, and players need to have belief in their coaches. Having belief in your teammates and coaches provides a sense that there's always hope, even when the circumstances may have others doubting. Belief helps to keep teams fighting, even when the odds are against them. Without belief, there would be no underdog victories, no dramatic upsets, no come-from-behind wins.

There's no shortage of teammates who lack belief in themselves. They don't think they have what it takes to come through in the clutch, make the play, or be a contributor to their team. They simply lack confidence in their abilities. However, if teammates express belief in that athlete who doubts him or herself, the chances of that person succeeding are better than if teammates express zero belief in that person. Just as my belief in God has made me better, teammates make each other (and the team) better when they believe in each other. Belief fosters confidence.

Principle:
I will choose to believe in my team, even when it's hard to do so.

CHAPTER 16

WATER TOWER

In the Summer of 1990, I went on a mission trip to Panama City Beach, Florida, with members of the Campus Outreach ministry from the University of Montevallo and Samford University. That summer, I made a friend who would impact my life dramatically in the following years. His name was Dennis Painter.

Dennis and I had competed against each other on the intramural fields at the University of Montevallo (we were in rival fraternities), but didn't really know each other until that mission trip. Dennis and I hit it off and became the best of friends. When the summer ended and we went back to campus, Dennis even offered to help me learn more about the Bible. He had been a Christian for much longer than me. I gladly accepted. We spent a lot of time together the rest of our college days.

Dennis and I didn't go out drinking like many other college students, but we did manage to create our own brand of mischief and fun. One evening, the two of us, along with great friends Chris Blansett and Danny Woodard, busted into an on-campus movie night and threw shaving-cream pies at fellow students (my belated apologies to the brunette on the third-row aisle seat). We also snuck onto the auditorium stage during an art-appreciation class while classical music played, and performed our very own ballet to entertain students in the class. Spending time with Dennis often meant adventure.

Dennis showed up at my dorm room late one night and said, "Throw on a swimsuit. I've got an adventure for us." Although I was already in bed, I got up, put on my swimsuit, and followed him out the door. We walked to the other side of campus in our swimsuits. Dennis carried a pillowcase, but wouldn't tell me what was in it. We started a trek into the woods on the far side of campus. I'd been on this path before. It led to an abandoned water tower on the edge of campus. Plenty of students, including myself, had jumped the fence surrounding it and climbed the ladder to the catwalk around the base of the water tank. It was an only-slightly-dangerous adventure to go on in small town Alabama.

My trip to the water tower this night was destined to be different, par for the course in a Dennis Painter adventure. Dennis and I climbed to the catwalk at the base of the tank, but then Dennis proceeded to climb a smaller ladder up the side of the tank to the very top. I'd never climbed this ladder before, so I didn't know what to expect. Dennis did. He'd obviously scouted it out and learned that there was a hatch on top of the sloped roof of the tank that was unlocked. The hatch had a bar holding it closed that only needed to be hit with a hammer a couple of times to be forced open. Dennis had brought a hammer in the pillowcase.

We opened the hatch, and Dennis pulled a flashlight out of the pillowcase and pointed a beam of light inside. We saw the tank had a ladder on the inside wall that started at the top of the tank and descended down into the dark water, which appeared to halfway fill the tank. I now knew why I was wearing a swimsuit.

Dennis used the shoulder strap of the flashlight to tie it to the ladder inside the tank. We spent the next thirty minutes or so jumping into the cold water from the top of the ladder and swimming around the inside. The water was cold, but seemed relatively clean. The inside of the tank was covered in rust that would easily fall off when you touched it. We'd hold our breath and count rungs on the ladder underneath the surface, seeing how far we could go down before touching the bottom. We never found the bottom. I think we were too afraid of what it might feel like if we touched it.

That night, Dennis and I created a memory that we've shared with countless others over the years. I don't know too many others who have swam in a water tower. I don't suggest doing it either, of course, but we all need a little adventure in our lives to really live!

LESSON

First off, you should never try to repeat what I did. Don't go try to find a water tower to climb or swim in. It's not worth the risk and is also against the law, I imagine.

Dennis played a big role in my life in my college years. He was a loyal friend. He was a mentor to me in my new-found faith. He spoke wisdom into my life. He encouraged me. He believed in me. He called me into adventure. These things all helped me not only enjoy my college experience, but also helped me become a better man. I'm so thankful for Dennis and friends like him I've had throughout my life.

I've done a pretty good job surrounding myself with friends and mentors who kept me out of severe trouble and helped me become a better version of myself. I fully believe that you become like those you spend the most time with, which is why it's so important that you choose your friends wisely. Your friends help forge your future.

TEAM APPLICATION

Like your family, you don't get to choose your team-mates, but you do get to choose who you spend the most time with. Do those you spend the most time with make you better? Do they act like wind in your sails to move you forward, or do they act like an anchor trying to hold you back? There is no neutral ground. If they're not helping you be better, they're holding you back.

There are lots of personalities on teams. You may not like some of them. You may love most of them. You need to spend time with all of them outside of practices and games in order to improve team chemistry. But, you must be selective about which teammates you spend the most time with. Do spend time with all of your teammates, but in that inner circle of three or five friends who you really lean into (who may or may not be on your team), be very selective.

Choosing your inner circle is one of the most important decisions you can make in your life. I once heard an NFL Hall of Famer say that before he started high school, he wrote out his vision statement, which stated all the things he wanted to achieve in life (which he later did achieve). His vision statement made it clear to him that if he wanted to achieve those things, he was going to have to change the friends he hung out with. He went to school and told his four buddies that he would no longer be hanging out with them. Those "buddies" threatened him, laughed at him, and even spread lies about him. But, this athlete was able to achieve what he did, in part, because of his choice to put distance between himself and those four guys.

Principle:
My friends help forge my future.

Dennis (right) and me on Panama City Beach,
Florida, the summer of 1990, where we first met

CHAPTER 17

COLLEGE BULLY

When I went off to college, I thought that my days of being bullied were behind me. However, even in college there are some who feel the need to bully others they believe are a threat to them. I had one significant bullying experience in college that I've never forgotten.

I began loving the sport of volleyball during my high school years. We didn't have a boys' volleyball team at Talladega High, but I played a lot at a summer camp I worked at during most of high school. When I went to college at the University of Montevallo, the Falcons had a really good women's volleyball program coached by Judy Green. I loved to go watch them play, and over the years I began helping out at some practices and calling lines during the home matches with one of my best friends and fraternity brothers, Bobby Deavers.

In the fall of 1990, the start of my junior year, a freshman volleyball player by the name of Shawna Sauls joined the team. Shawna was a tall, athletic, blonde-haired, blue-eyed stunner who would catch anyone's eye. She certainly caught mine. Apparently I caught hers, as well, and before long we started spending some time together and dating. The relationship wasn't meant to be, however, and we both knew it. We ended things on a really good note and remained good friends, something I wish I could say about all my previous relationships.

Shawna had plenty of suitors, and it wasn't long before she dated someone else on campus, a baseball player. I knew of him, since it was a small campus, but I'd never spoken to him. That was about to change now that the two of them were dating.

Our school's cafeteria wasn't large, and most groups of people, like fraternities, sororities, and sports teams, all seemed to have tables where they always sat. All the baseball players usually sat together in a particular section of the cafeteria. In order for me to return my cafeteria tray to the dishwasher, I had to pass through the tables where the baseball team sat. One day, after I dropped my tray off, Shawna's new boyfriend called my name as I walked past. He then said with a raised voice, so that all his baseball buddies sitting around him could hear, "Stay away from Shawna!" I tried my best to ignore him and continued my walk to the exit.

Now, I should mention that although Shawna's new boyfriend wasn't taller than me, he was significantly thicker (from years spent in the weight room, no doubt). I found him intimidating, for sure, and I certainly felt physically threatened by him. Flat out, I was scared. It was like I was in high school all over again, when guys felt like they had to use their muscles to have their way and gain respect. Regardless, I knew that I'd have to be careful to keep my distance from Shawna so as to not give this guy a reason to jump me.

That evening, I was in the cafeteria eating by myself, which usually never happened. Guess who walks in and wants to join me at my table? Shawna! The first thing I did was start looking over my shoulder to see if I was about to get jumped from behind. I realized the coast was clear, but I remember being very rude to Shawna. I didn't tell her what her boyfriend had said, but instead of being a gentleman and treating her with respect, I was rude to her. I don't recall what I said—I know it wasn't much—but I remember her saying, "What's wrong with you?" To which I replied, "Nothing. I'm just having a bad day and don't want to talk."

She got up and left, which made me feel a little safer, but I soon felt horrible about how I'd acted. Shawna was a friend of mine, and she certainly didn't deserve to be treated the way I'd just treated her, regardless of how it might impact the safety of my face. I let my fear of this bully cause me to disrespect a friend. It was not a proud moment for me.

I didn't sleep much that night. I knew what needed to be done, and it scared me to death. I spoke to my friend Dennis to get some advice, or maybe a second opinion, and he confirmed what I already thought. I was going to have to confront the bully.

I knew what dorm the baseball players lived in, since it was right next to mine. I looked up his room number in the school directory, and I went to talk to him (at best, that's all that would happen). As I began walking down the hall to his dorm room, I saw him and one of his teammates moving a big metal desk from one dorm room to another. He was wearing a white undershirt and athletic shorts. His biceps bulged from that T-shirt as if to say, "You want a piece of me?" I didn't pay for a gun show, but I sure was getting one!

My mouth was as dry as a sunbaked cotton ball. I approached and asked if I could speak to him in private. He said, "Yeah. Give me a second." After he finished moving the desk, he led me into his room and stood in front of me, waiting for me to speak.

I nervously rambled out some words—something along the lines of me posing no threat to him and Shawna, but that I didn't want to feel like I had to be disrespectful to her. I just wanted to remain her friend. He seemed okay with what I said and agreed that there was no reason she and I couldn't be friends. I offered my hand, he shook it, and I left.

I felt such a huge sense of relief come over me as I walked back to my dorm room. As much as I still hate confrontation, if you find the courage to stand up to the bully and survive, it sure can boost your self-confidence. I'm not quite sure how my body fit through the doorway when I got back to my dorm room, because I'm certain I grew bigger and wider during the short walk from his room to mine!

Shawna and I remained good friends. She later found out what the guy had said to me, and she wasn't happy with him. Their relationship didn't last long. I occasionally crossed paths with him on campus, and we'd give a little head nod to each other. I think I earned his respect that day, and who knows? Maybe I showed him a better way to handle himself in the future.

I actually played on a softball team with him for a short while a year or so later. We never were chummy, but we were respectful to each other.

LESSON

I've often heard it said that the best way to deal with a bully is to stand up to him or her. I'm a pretty firm believer in that. It may not always turn out the way you'd like, but the regret that comes from being too afraid to face the bully hurts much longer than a black eye or bruised ego. Is it scary? Heck yes! Can it be dangerous? Absolutely! But, in the right situation, it can change you for the better, as it was for me in this story.

If I had to guess, I think my college bully knew he'd outkicked his coverage when he started dating Shawna. He likely felt I might damage the good thing he had a loose hold of. He was insecure in his relationship. If he could demonstrate his physical power over me, especially in front of all his teammates, it would help him feel more secure. It's easy for me to see it now, but it wasn't back then.

What's strange is that the bully caused me to bully Shawna, in a sense. I'd just been disrespected, and I turned right around and disrespected someone myself. I needed to stand up to my bully so I wouldn't feel the need to bully Shawna. Having the courage to stand up to this guy was a very proud moment in my life. That day was a win for me—I stripped him of his power over me—and Shawna won, as well, since she would no longer be bullied by me.

TEAM APPLICATION

A good team should function like a healthy family. They should be loyal to each other, always supporting, encouraging, protecting, and caring for the needs of one another. In this story, Shawna was my teammate—she was my friend—and I should strive to protect my teammates. Funny thing is, she needed me to protect her from me. Because of her boyfriend's threat, I'd just mistreated her, and likely would have continued to do so if things hadn't changed.

Shawna needed a teammate to go to bat for her. She'd done no wrong and yet received something she didn't deserve. I needed to go to bat for Shawna, which scared me, because I wasn't sure if it would lead to me getting pounded or not. But, I was the one who had the power to make things better for her. I'm so glad I was able to be a loyal teammate in that situation.

During the life of your team, you will have teammates who will need someone to go to bat for them. They'll need support for something they're going through or some adversity they're facing. You need to be there for them. You need to be there for *any* of them, not just your best friend on the team. That might mean you stand up for them when someone disrespects them, sit with them in the cafeteria, encourage them after that horrible mistake they made, or be patient with them when they don't catch on to the new play right away during practice. A lot of teams like to talk about being a family as part of their team culture. It's easy to talk about; it's much harder to live it.

Principle:
My team is my family, and I will treat them that way.

CHAPTER 18

FIRST YEAR OF MARRIAGE

I'd always heard people say that the first year of marriage is hard, but I wasn't sold on that. There's no way my wife, Hope, and I would ever have a hard year of marriage . . . especially not the first year! All of that newlywed love and excitement was going to make our first year of marriage amazing. Not! Add me to the long list of seasoned married people who advise the youngsters that the first year of marriage is going to be difficult.

I take full blame for the difficulties of our first year of marriage. Maybe Hope has some blame to take in there somewhere, but if so, I haven't found it yet. Nope. I think this was all on me. Let me explain.

I'm proud to have been born and raised in Alabama, and when I was young, I had no plans to live anywhere else. My comfort zone was in Alabama, and that's where I intended to stay. Hope, on the other hand, was born and raised in the northwest suburbs of Chicago. To be quite honest, Chicago intimidated me. From all I'd heard, I thought Chicago was filled with violence, wind, traffic, Yankees, high prices, and homelessness. So, when Hope and I began discussing the prospects of marriage, I made it adamantly clear that I was never going to live in Chicago. Here's some advice: never say never!

Hope seemed fully on board with the idea of living in Alabama and raising a family there. We were married in Illinois on June 4, 1994, and I whisked her away to sweet home Alabama to begin our life together. She found an entry-level job working as a bank teller in Mountain Brook, an affluent suburb of Birmingham, while months prior I had landed a good job with a promising future. We lived in an apartment in Hoover, also a suburb of Birmingham.

I had graduated from the University of Montevallo in December of 1992, and had been living with roommates up until the time I got the apartment that Hope and I would share once we were married. I played a lot of slow-pitch softball during that time. On weekends in the warm-weather months, I played in tournaments with a pretty competitive team, and I played in a couple of leagues during the week. When Hope and I returned from our honeymoon, I went right back to working and playing softball like I always had. I brought Hope along to cheer me on, but also so she could meet some of my friends and their wives and girlfriends. Hope is fairly introverted, so I was doing what I could to help her create a network of friends in her new environment.

Then came the injury. Not to me, but to Hope. To really know Hope is to know that she has a serious phobia of rodents (living, dead, or fake). One day while working in a small drive-through building at the bank, Hope saw a mouse on the floor. She freaked out and tried to hop up onto a floor safe. Her vertical jump was lacking, and she fell and badly injured her knee. It was so bad that it required her to miss work, get fluid drained from the knee, and be laid up on the couch for a few weeks in lots of pain. She could only walk with the help of crutches.

Now, you'd think this is the part of the story where I

play the devoted, loving husband who puts everything else aside to care for my injured wife. I would prepare her food, stay with her, fluff her pillow, help her to the bathroom, and comfort her as best I could. If only I would've done some of that. Instead, what I did was continue to travel to play softball tournaments every weekend and three nights a week, leaving Hope laid up on the couch by herself. Yep, this first year of marriage was going to be great!

Needless to say, it's hard to keep a wife—or anyone—happy if you continually put your own needs before theirs. But, I had teammates counting on me to track down fly balls in the outfield and to score runs. I had made a commitment to those teams well before June 4, 1994, so shouldn't I live up to those commitments regardless? The idiot part of my brain thought I should, and unfortunately, the idiot part of my brain won out.

Hope missed her family and everything familiar to her in Illinois, and now she was forced to miss her new husband, as well. This type of existence wasn't going to last long. After only seven months of marriage, guess what I was doing? Moving to Roselle, Illinois, with Hope to live with her parents. When I said I was never going to live in Chicago many months prior, I also meant the suburbs!

Never say never.

The move north was supposed to be temporary, and we planned to move back down south after Hope was mentally ready. But, after twenty-five years of living in Illinois, I'm beginning to think it's going to be permanent.

LESSON

I fully own the mistake I made in this story. I failed to

put the needs of my wife before my own desires. I don't think it's possible to have happy, healthy relationships if you're always getting your way and not willing to put others first sometimes. As counterintuitive as it may seem, putting the needs of others before your own makes for a more satisfying life. Not only does serving others make you feel better; those you serve actually want to serve you more often.

Maybe it's because I'd been living on my own for over a couple years, and I wasn't used to putting someone else's needs before my own, but I think the bigger reason for my selfishness may have been due to the success I had in softball. Don't get me wrong—I wasn't a professional-caliber player, but I was pretty stinking good. I was usually the fastest person on whatever team I played on, could track down most any fly ball in the outfield, and I could usually hit for average and with some power. People wanted me to be on their team. Teammates would be disappointed if I couldn't show up for some reason, which was very seldom. It felt great to be wanted. It felt great to be one of the best on the team. It felt great to have others celebrate my accomplishments. I wasn't used to all that, so it felt amazing! I placed my identity in being a great softball player and a valued teammate.

Unfortunately, I wasn't willing to let Hope's injury get in the way of me identifying as a great softball player. God sure seems to have a way of helping us adjust our priorities. I'm sure there could have been a balance between being a good husband and a softball player in Alabama, but I wasn't willing to find that balance at the time, so it was taken from me. With the change in geography, I was no longer a part of three teams. I was forced to focus on putting the "home team" before the softball team. I did play softball again for a number of years after moving to Illinois, but only for one team at a time, and always locally.

TEAM APPLICATION

I've been married for twenty-five years now, and I still have to be reminded sometimes that it's not all about me. When you join a sports team, you may also need to be reminded that it's not all about you. Even if you're the best on the team, even if you're the one mentioned in all the articles, even if your parents or guardians tell you so, *it's not all about you.* I tell student-athletes that when they commit to be on a team, they're giving up their individual rights. I tell them they can think about their needs 1 percent of the time, but the needs of the team should be their focus the other 99 percent. Harsh? I don't think so.

So many athletes have spent their young lives being conditioned by the crowd. Here's just two of what can be several things that cause athletes to be conditioned by the crowd:

1. When a player makes a great play in youth sports (gets the hit, scores the goal, makes the basket, scores the touchdown, etc.), the crowd cheers in celebration. The athlete loves it! Because it feels great, the athlete wants more of it. So, the athlete works hard to record the individual statistics so they can once again be celebrated. The things they may do that show themselves to be a selfless teammate (i.e. passing the ball, setting the screen, encouraging an upset teammate) don't get celebrated by the crowd.

2. If a parent misses a game, the first question they usually ask their child is, "How'd you do?" They want to hear about their kid's playing time and

statistics more than they do about whether or not the team won. So, parents are reinforcing to the player that their individual statistics are more important than the success of the team.

With these and other influences, it's hard for student-athletes to have a team-first mentality—to be a we-before-me type of player. Coaches may spend a lot of time and energy teaching their players the importance of putting the team needs first—to play harder for the name on the front of the jersey than the name on the back of it. If a teammate can put the name on the front of the jersey first, the name on the back of the jersey always receives its fair reward.

Principle:
I focus on being the best player for the team,
not the best player on the team.

Our wedding photo
June 4, 1994

CHAPTER 19

SAMMY

My older brother, Sammy, and I were only separated in age by thirteen months. Despite being very similar in age, we were very different people. As the first-born son, he was named after my father. It was appropriate, since Sammy strongly resembled our dad and the Williams side of the family. The name wouldn't have fit me as well, because I took more after my mom's side of the family and really don't have much in common with my father.

Perhaps the biggest difference between Sammy and I was the way we approached life. Sammy always held out hope that our family would be reunited, and when it didn't, it made him angry, and he had a hard time moving forward with anything else in life. Early on, I hoped to be reunited with my family, as well, but I quickly realized it wasn't going to happen. I tried my best to be thankful for what I had and make the best of my situation.

Because Sammy and I were very different people, our relationship was almost always on the rocks. We fought a lot. By that, I mean he pushed and beat on me a lot. Not severe beatings, just those body punches here and there to remind me of his physical dominance. I felt the wrath of his anger often.

As Sammy grew and developed behavioral issues, Martha had a very hard time trying to parent him. Sammy didn't want Martha to parent him. He rebelled against her every chance he got, reminding her that she was not his mother and couldn't boss him around. Martha tried putting him in therapy and on medications, but nothing seemed to help. She even considered enrolling him at a ranch for troubled kids, but he refused to stay there after we visited, and she refused to force it on him.

In middle school, Sammy tried living with other people. He'd find a friend whose parents would allow him to stay with them for a while. What he learned was that those friends also had parents with rules, and they wouldn't put up with his disrespect and bad behavior, either. These experiments only lasted a short while until he was forced to move back in with us, often promising to be different, but never holding true to that.

He smoked, drank, used drugs, and was sexually active very early in life. He snuck out of the house so often that Martha had to put an alarm on the door that would go off if the doorknob moved. He started sneaking out of the windows after that.

Sammy's rebellion made me feel sorry for Martha. She loved him and just wanted to help him any way she could. His actions broke her heart, and she cried over him a lot. Sammy took advantage of Martha's mercy. I often heard her tell him he wasn't welcome back in the house (trying to exercise tough love), only to welcome him back when he was down on his luck and needed help. Even though he often stole money from her, she continued to try to help him financially when she saw a strong need, which there always was.

Sammy dropped out of high school after his sophomore

year. By this time, he was living in apartments around town or with friends, and only coming back home when he needed something. He needed a job to earn money, but because he wasn't willing to obey authority, he never lasted long. I could count about thirty places in Talladega where he'd been employed at some point.

Sammy chose to get married at the age of sixteen to a high school classmate pregnant with someone else's baby. That marriage was a short one and ended July 21, 1986, just five months after the baby was born. He'd soon re-marry again. His new wife already had a son, but it wasn't long before they had their own child, Jessica.

Despite all the horrible decisions Sammy made in his life, he got something right with Jessica. She's grown to be an amazing wife and mother to two beautiful girls. I'm so proud of who she's become. I'll never forget when Jessica's mom divorced Sammy, and he drove over to our house and parked his crappy brown car under the oak tree we used to climb. He opened the hatchback and laid out pictures of Jessica all over the floor of the trunk, sobbing like a baby as he looked at them. He loved Jessica more than anything, and the thought of not getting to spend time with her broke his heart.

A long sufferer of depression, Sammy's suicide attempts began in middle school. Initially I never considered them to be suicide attempts, but rather cries for attention. Attempts started with overdosing on over-the-counter medications. He was such a strong guy, though, that the early attempts never seemed to bother his body much. He'd just sleep it off, and there'd never seem to be any long-lasting impact from the overdose.

One day after coming home from my summer job in 1989, about a month after Sammy's divorce from his second wife, Martha met me at the door crying. Sammy was lying on the living room floor, and she couldn't wake him up. I went inside and tried to wake him, and he came to for about a second before blacking out again.

I was pissed. I was mad that he didn't even live with us at the time, and he chose to come over to our house to overdose. I know this was a horrible thought, but for years I'd been seeing what his actions were doing to Martha, the one person who'd always been there for him. This was his third suicide attempt in the last ten days!

I told Martha we should just let him sleep it off like he always did. She called the hospital to tell them what type of pills Sammy had overdosed on. They said we should get him to the hospital right away, since those particular pills could cause his heart to stop.

I somehow got him up to his feet and into a car, then drove him to the ER. They pumped his stomach at the hospital, and he rebounded like he always did. This attempt landed him in a doctor-ordered stint at a mental institution on June 14. He stayed there for a couple weeks, I believe, but it did him no good. Doctors tried different medications to treat his depression, but nothing ever seemed to help.

When I came home to visit during my last couple years of college, I always made sure to visit Sammy. Martha told me how my visits always seemed to cheer him up. I knew they did, and I enjoyed my time with him. The visits with him during my last couple years of college were some of my favorite times with Sammy. During those years, our relationship was much different and much better. He was proud of what I was accomplishing in my life, and it was as if he looked up to me, like I was the big brother in our relationship. He regretted all the bad decisions he'd made in his life and was proud that I'd chosen a different path.

After I became a Christian in college, I shared my new faith with him during one of my visits home. Although he respected my decision, he said he couldn't believe there was a God. He said, "If there was a God, he wouldn't have given me this life I've had to live." It was a sad statement, and he meant it. And, despite my faith, I could understand it. I might feel the same if I were in his shoes.

After I graduated college, I never moved back to Talladega. I married in 1994, and after a short stint in Birmingham with my wife, we moved to the Chicago suburbs. I was thankful that Sammy and I were able to create a very good relationship while I was in college—so much so that I asked him to be the best man in my wedding. He did a great job! It was nice having a relationship with him where I didn't end up getting punched. We were adults now, and it certainly seemed to help our relationship.

I realized the suicide attempts were getting more serious when Sammy drank antifreeze. He'd heard about dogs drinking it and the antifreeze killing them pretty quick. However, it didn't accomplish what he was hoping for. He was hospitalized again as the antifreeze began working to destroy his kidneys. He lost a lot of weight and strength, but yet again, his body rebounded from the damage he'd done.

On one of my visits from Chicago to visit Martha, I was floored at the sight of him. He had lost so much weight from his hospitalization, he was flat-out skinny. He had never been fat, just strong, but he was far from that now.

During our visit, I challenged him to arm-wrestle me. Sammy and I arm-wrestled a lot growing up, and he always beat me easily. On this day, I felt I finally had a chance to win. And, win I did! It was the most shallow victory I think I've ever had in my life. I felt so horrible afterward. His face looked as defeated as his weakened body. I'd already bested him in education, in relationships, in work, in love. Did I really have to take from him the one thing he'd always had over me—his strength? For some reason, I guess I did. I wish I could have a do-over on that one. I'm sorry, brother.

Around 8:00 p.m. on October 16, 1998, the phone rang. I was playing video games with my brother-in-law, Brian. He and his wife, Heather, were in town to see our first-born child, Cooper, who was a month old. On the line was Brenda Kent, a special friend to Martha who lived down the street in Talladega. I'll never forget her words: "Well . . . he finally did it." I knew what that meant.

Brenda was at Martha's house when she called to tell me Sammy had just committed suicide under Martha's carport. He'd come back home to end his life.

Excerpt from Sammy's suicide note

LESSON

There are so many things that you can take from the life that Sammy lived and the relationship that we had. I'll choose to make one point, and that point is, one plus one does not always equal two. Let me explain.

For generations, the men in the Williams family have been less than stellar. Alcoholism has been the main reason for that. I'm not here to share their story, but I do know this: when my wife, Hope, and I found out we'd be having a boy, I called Martha from Chicago with excitement to tell her the news. Sammy had never had a son, and I knew that my son, Cooper, would be the first boy to carry on the Williams name. After I shared this news with her, Martha replied with the most serious tone in her voice, "I don't know if that's a name you want to carry on."

I responded with confidence, "I'm creating a new breed of Williamses."

I've been working like heck to be different than how my family history might dictate I should turn out. If you look up statistics regarding fatherless boys, you would see that Sammy became another statistic in many ways. I did not. Why? I made very different choices than Sammy, and I thank him for helping me to do that. I watched all the negative consequences of his decisions and wanted different for myself. In a way, it's almost like Sammy sacrificed his life for me. If I didn't have his example to look at, my choices and decisions may have been very different.

I recently heard of a term used in the field of psychology that I feel describes me: transitional character. A transitional character is someone who changes the direction of a lineage. They grow up in an emotionally damaging environment, yet somehow are able to withstand the damage and avoid passing the damage down to their own children. I'm trying my best to be a transitional character. I'm trying to change the course of history for my family. I make plenty of mistakes, and my wife and kids have had to suffer from them, but I'm committed to making sure they never have to go through what Sammy, my mother, my father, and I did. My kids will be better prepared to continue changing the history of the Williams name.

I've worked with a lot of kids from broken homes and horrible family histories. Unfortunately, history repeats itself quite often. The majority of these kids have grown up to repeat history and let the damage flow on down the family line. One plus one does not have to equal two! Just because statistics say you should turn out this way, or suffer with this, or struggle with that, doesn't mean that has to be true in your life. You can buck the trend. You can break the mold!

Don't let a statistic choose your fate. You choose it.

TEAM APPLICATION

Every player and every team must deal with expectations placed by themselves or by others. Players usually have expectations for their game performance that are often unrealistic. Teams can go into a season with expectations of how much they will achieve during the season. These expectations can be dangerous, because they may apply undue pressure on the team and individual players, or it may instill some limiting beliefs on the players.

Here are a couple of examples to illustrate the dangers:

- *Expectation*: Sean expects to rush for two touchdowns every game during his senior season.

o *Problem*: Sean has placed an expectation on himself that he can't control. He can't control how others block for him, how the opponents defend against the run, or how healthy he might be during a game. Will he sacrifice the needs of the team to "get his"? If he fails to meet his own expectations, will he still be a good teammate? Will he turn the ball over on first and goal at the two-yard line stretching for his touchdown, or will he secure the ball and live to play the next play?

- *Expectation*: In every preseason article, the team is picked to finish last in conference the upcoming season.

  o *Problem*: Although some players and teams will see this as a challenge, many will see this as a foregone conclusion. It can become a self-fulfilling prophesy, especially if the season gets off to a bad start. The players can believe the press and lack the belief that they can be any different than everyone expects.

Teams need to abandon expectations. Teams need to focus on the things within their control that they can do to be their best. They can't buy into what the naysayers and doubters are saying about them. Regardless of what the statistics say should happen during the course of a game or a season, players must stay focused on what they can control.

Principle:
One plus one does not have to equal two.

National Suicide Prevention Lifeline: 1-800-273-8255

Sammy (right) serving as my best man on my wedding day

CHAPTER 20

ABS DIET CHAMPION

In the winter of 2004, I'd had enough. I'd been neglecting my physical fitness and showing no discipline in my diet. I was easily finding excuses to avoid working out and eating right. I was having lower-back pain, I didn't feel like going to the gym, and my wife was pregnant with our third child, Hudson. She was gaining weight (obviously), so why couldn't I gain a little "sympathy weight," as well?

Historically, I go through hills and valleys of motivation when it comes to fitness. I'll sometimes be relentless in the gym and disciplined in my diet for a couple of months, and then I'll go through a valley where all that self-control goes out the window. Sound familiar?

I'd been on a work trip and bought a health magazine at the airport to read on my flight home. Once again, I'd decided to rededicate myself to my fitness, and I was hoping to find some good work-out ideas. While flipping through the pages, I saw an ad for a diet competition. They claimed you could follow their diet for six weeks to get six-pack abs like a supermodel. I thought, *Yeah, right. There's no way!* Despite my disbelief in their claim, I decided to participate in the challenge for two reasons: One, I hoped it would help inspire me to get in better shape, and two, I wanted to prove the ad wrong.

The contest was one of those typical before-and-after-photo-type contests that you see in many fitness magazines. The contest was starting in January of 2005, so until that time I continued to eat any and everything I wanted, ballooning my weight up to the heaviest I've ever been. Although I doubt anyone would have called me fat, it wasn't a good weight or look for my relatively thin frame.

When the contest began, I was totally bought in. I subscribed to their online meal plans, where I could print out a grocery-shopping list and have each and every meal specified for me. They also provided the work-out plan I was to follow. I committed myself fully to trying to prove that ad wrong. I even avoided cheat meals when the diet permitted it. I had one small sugar cookie on Valentine's Day, but that was the only semblance of junk food I ate during the six-week challenge.

The workouts were really tough, to the point that I got nauseous a number of times during the first couple of weeks. Several years prior, I had built a gym in my garage in order to spend more time at home with my first two kids, Cooper and Hadley, instead of spending my evenings at the gym. Despite very cold conditions in my unheated garage, I never skipped a workout and followed the instructions for each one religiously. I've always been good at following directions, so that's simply what I was committed to do: follow the directions with all I had.

After three weeks, I took another picture of myself. It was far from amazing. I certainly saw improvement, but again, I thought that there was no way the supermodel abs were possible with only three weeks to go. Despite being a little discouraged, I continued to give my all for the next three weeks.

The next three weeks made a big difference! I lost a lot more body fat, and the abs looked pretty good—not supermodel amazing, but it was quite a transformation. I took my final photo and submitted it. I told Hope that I'd be disappointed if I didn't make the top ten, because I doubted that there were ten people in the country who had worked harder than I had during those six weeks.

Well, I did indeed get selected by editors of the magazine to be among the top-ten finalists in the country. Mission accomplished! It was so exciting to see my hard work get rewarded. The top-ten finalists were posted on a website where the public voted to determine a final three.

Fortunately for me at the time, I worked for a very large Fortune 500 company. Coworkers circulated an email with a link to vote for me to branch offices all over the country. I'd pass people I'd never met in the hallways wishing me luck and saying they'd voted for me. Although it was a bit embarrassing to know that coworkers had seen pictures of me with my shirt off (especially the before picture), it felt great to be supported by so many.

When online voting was complete, I was told that I'd made it to the final round of three contestants. I was thrilled! The contest winner would now be chosen by the editors of the magazine from the final three. I had to submit a short essay about my experience during the challenge and also be interviewed by one of the magazine editors.

On June 5, 2005 (my birthday), I received a phone call informing me that I'd been chosen as the winner! I was ecstatic! I couldn't believe it. I knew that my hard work and results proved that I was deserving, but I never set out thinking I would win. The prize for my efforts: a brand-new sports car. Not bad for a guy looking to prove an ad wrong!

LESSON

I don't share this story to brag about my accomplishments. I share this story because I truly did learn a valuable lesson during this competition. I'd certainly worked pretty hard in my life at times, both in the gym and in my various jobs, but during that six-week challenge, I pushed myself harder physically and dieted with more discipline than I'd done at any time in my life.

Prior to this challenge, I feel like my overall work ethic was pretty average. If things got too uncomfortable, I'd back off the intensity to regain comfort. Our brain seeks comfort for us, and way too often I listened to my brain instead of pushing myself out of my comfort zone. I had settled for average a lot in life. This challenge taught me that I didn't have to settle for average. If I was going to exceed "average" in anything, then I was going to have to work much harder than I was used to, and embrace greater discomfort. I no longer wanted to settle.

Embracing discomfort is no easy task for most individuals. People commonly try to avoid discomfort, but if you avoid discomfort, you postpone growth. Whether it's in the gym, in your sport, at school, at work, or in relationships, we have to get uncomfortable in order to improve ourselves and achieve greater success in those areas of our lives. I feel like many years of my life were spent underachieving because of my desire to stay comfortable. Life is far too short and far too valuable to spend any period of time underachieving.

TEAM APPLICATION

The human brain is always seeking comfort for us. This is great in some instances, but for student-athletes, this fact means that they must often battle their minds when it comes to pushing themselves to prepare for competition. Coaches are asking their players to give their all, but the players' minds are telling them to shut it down when they start to get taxed. It's a constant battle for most athletes.

Some athletes will join a team thinking they understand what it means to work hard, only to be shocked with how much is demanded of them. They thought they worked hard before, but soon realize they hadn't pushed themselves nearly hard enough. They have to learn a new definition of hard work.

I know from my own personal experiences and from working with many athletes that when we start to get tired, the brain sends us a message saying, "Stop! You can't go anymore. You have to rest!" I also know that our bodies will go much farther than our brain wants us to believe. The brain seeks safety and comfort, which is great in the right setting, but not when you're trying to develop strength and endurance. So, the brain is telling us that we need to shut it down well before we actually have to.

Athletes with better conditioning than their opponents improve their chances of winning. If we're going to out-work our competition, then we need to ignore the messages from the brain, embrace the discomfort, and keep pushing.

I've heard that when a storm approaches, the buffalo walks into the storm so it gets through it more quickly. Cows, on the other hand, walk away from storms, delaying the effect the storm is going to have on them. Don't be a cow. Be a buffalo.

Principle:
If I avoid discomfort, I postpone growth.

My oldest son, Cooper, and me
posing next to a Ford Mustang

CHAPTER 21

TOUGH MUDDER

While online one day in 2011, I saw an advertisement for Tough Mudder, an obstacle-course race company whose events are largely centered around getting as muddy as possible. I clicked on the link to check out their website and was enamored with the idea almost instantly. Now in my forties, I saw this as a fun way to test myself. I was confident that I could complete such a course, but I wanted to see how well I could do it.

I recruited some friends through my church to join me at the Tough Mudder event in a couple months' time. Before I knew it, there were twelve of us committed to participate. I was the elder statesman of the group, with most of the guys being ten-to-fifteen years younger than me. Most of us were in decent shape, but we agreed we'd better start training for an event like this.

Since the race was my idea and I had recruited most everyone, I took charge of scheduling a few training dates for the group on Saturday mornings at a local forest preserve. We ran trails and hills, doing anything we could think to do with little equipment to help us get in better shape. Most of the group members showed up on these training dates, but of course everyone needed to be training on their own throughout each week to really make a difference in their fitness levels.

Included in the twelve were Jon, Jason, Tommy, Greg, Brian, Ryan, Jeff, Mike, and Jordan. I had met a few of these guys when they were in the high school church youth group with which I helped out. Others I had met through a new church we recently helped start. The last one to join the group was a guy named Ian, who went to our church and maybe was the least athletic of all of us. Yet, he was excited to join the group, and we welcomed him with open arms. We told him he'd better start getting in shape right away, as race day was soon approaching.

Race day came quickly, and most of us piled into two cars to get everyone to the event. Ian drove solo and met the rest of us there. We would be competing in an open wave, which meant we weren't looking to win the event; we were just a group of guys looking to have fun.

It was a beautiful morning for a race! We went through the check-in process, wrote our race numbers on our foreheads, and walked around a bit before we needed to be at the starting line. We also had our twelfth guy meet us there. I don't recall his name—he was a friend of one of the guys—but I do recall that he was dressed like Fred Flintstone. We were all getting excited as we waited for our heat to be called over the loudspeaker.

In most every race I've been in, dating back to my high school track season, I always come out of the gate strong—often too strong. The adrenaline is pumping and I'm feeling great, so I just take off at a clip that can't be sustained for long. As our group left the starting line, I think we all made the mistake of going out a little too quickly. We all felt good, though, and it appeared that our training had paid off. Well, except for Ian, who I doubt ever spent any time training.

The first part of the race was a pretty flat quarter-mile run. Then, we had to start climbing over large hay bales going up one of the ski-slopes on the mountain the event was held at. Ian was struggling before we ever thought about climbing over hay bales. His breathing was way too hard for the first mile of a ten-to-twelve-mile course. Soon after the start, he had to stop to catch his breath while the rest of us chomped at the bit to keep moving to the next obstacle.

As the organizer of the group, I felt responsible for Ian. I encouraged the others to slow down and wait for Ian to catch his breath. Initially, they did. But, each time Ian needed to stop and catch his breath, the others grew more and more impatient. He obviously didn't train like the rest of us had. I understood the others' feelings. Why would we want to let one person slow down the entire group? Yet, I felt a loyalty toward Ian, and I didn't want to just cut him loose on mile one.

Jason and Jordan reminded me that they both had to get back home for events they were committed to in Chicago later that evening, and there was no way we would be able to finish the race in time for them to make their commitments at the pace that Ian was traveling. I knew they were right. We had to leave Ian behind, or else the event was going to be a bust for all of us. I had to have the hard conversation with Ian. He was sad to hear we would no longer wait for him, but he also understood. I worried about Ian for the next few miles. He had wanted to fit in with the group, to belong. I identified with that in a lot of ways and would have hated to be left behind if the shoe were on the other foot.

After we left Ian behind, the group had a great time going through the various obstacles on the course. We crawled under barbed wire in the mud, climbed steep ski slopes, helped each other over walls and cargo nets, and carried heavy logs while wading through ponds. It was a blast! It certainly got more challenging the farther into the course we got. None of us had really trained to endure that long of a distance, so we really had to gut it out the last few miles. But, we all finished proudly, even Ian. Ian told us the next day at church that although it took him six hours, he did finish. I was proud of him for not quitting, and apologized again that we had left him behind. He was very forgiving.

Soon after the Tough Mudder event, I got an idea that I felt was given to me from God. I'd received such positive benefits from that event, and I wanted others to get the opportunity to feel the same thing. I thought maybe I could start a company that provided similar experiences, where we'd focus on testing our bodies and challenging our character during the events. After all, we rely on our character much more often in our lives than we rely on our physical strength or endurance.

I started Battle-Tested in the Fall of 2012 to do just that: to help individuals become better by challenging their muscles, minds, and morals. It was a mission that really scared me. I'd never started a company before. Could I even do something like that? I wasn't so sure, but God gave me just enough courage to take small steps to give it a try.

Battle-Tested looks very different today than how I originally planned it to be, and I'm quite okay with that. Battle-Tested is now a nonprofit, and I get the opportunity to serve high school and college sport teams through team- and character-building events aimed to prepare student-athletes for greater success in their sport and in life. I get to help prepare thousands of students each year for the battles they're going to face in life. I'm so blessed by each and every opportunity that Battle-Tested provides me to impact others.

I used to think that Battle-Tested might be the next Tough Mudder. I'm glad it's not the next Tough Mudder, but the first Battle-Tested.

LESSON

That day we did the Tough Mudder event, my buddies and I challenged ourselves, and we all conquered the challenge. I personally came out on the other side of the challenge with greater confidence in my abilities. I've learned that when I subject myself to physical difficulties/discomfort/challenges like I did that day, then the everyday difficulties I face in life seem like nothing. For me, overcoming obstacles in the physical realm helps me to overcome challenges in other areas of my life.

It may sound silly, but I became a better version of myself on that muddy course that day. When I finished the course, my body was covered in mud, grass, grime, bruises, and a little blood. The shower afterward was amazing! After all was washed off, it revealed a better Blake.

However, the real lesson from this story relates to Ian. As I said, Ian wanted to belong in our group. The problem is, he didn't do what was needed in order to belong. He hadn't adequately prepared himself for the commitment that he'd made. He did work hard and was able to finish the race that day, but at the pace he deserved based on his preparation.

For a long while after the event, I struggled over the

moral dilemma I faced of leaving Ian behind. Had I done the right thing? Should I have let the rest of the group run ahead, then stay and help Ian through the rest of the course by myself? I've come to the conclusion that I did do the right thing, but maybe not on purpose. The main reason I left Ian was because my selfish desire to run the race with some of my best friends (at my desired pace) won out over my desire to be loyal to a guy I'd only recently met. I admit, it was a selfish decision. Despite the motive, the decision turned out to be the right one. Ian told me he learned so much about himself all alone on the course that day. He was able to learn his own valuable lessons that he likely wouldn't have learned by having me or the entire group stay with him and "carry" him through the course.

We all became Tough Mudders that day!

TEAM APPLICATION

Let me make an assumption about your team. On your team, there's at least one player who isn't getting the playing time he or she feels they deserve. Perhaps this athlete feels he or she should be starting the game or playing a more desirable position. Chances are, there's more than one player who feels this way. It's from the mouths of these players that we may hear the following statements:

- "Coach doesn't like me."
- "Coach likes him/her better than me."
- "It's political."
- "I'm not fully back from my injury."

These statements are just excuses. There's a chance these statements might hold some truth in very rare circumstances, but if a player really deserved more playing time, they'd be getting it. I don't think anyone wants to win more than coaches (their jobs are often on the line), and they're going to make decisions they think give their team the best chance to win. Not all players (or their parents) will agree with those decisions. That's okay. You don't have to like the decision, but you need to respect it.

If you're not getting the playing time you want, then my guess is that you're simply not performing well enough—on or off the field—to earn it. Being named a starter or getting more playing time usually is the result of a lot of hard work done over a long period of time. In other words, it's earned. A good coach won't give a player the starting position just because he or she wants it; the athlete has to earn it.

There are starters and nonstarters on every team for a reason. The starters have earned the right to start, and the nonstarters usually have not. You've earned the role on the team that you currently have. If you want a different role, I suggest asking the coach how you need to improve in order to get it. If the coach provides feedback that lets you know a greater role might be possible, then get to work to improve for that possibility. If your coach's feedback doesn't give you hope for a greater role, then be thankful for the role you have and don't complain about what you don't have.

Principle:
*I won't always get what I want,
but I'll usually get what I deserve.*

*A photo taken early into our Tough Mudder event
when we still had Ian (second from right) with us.
I'm sixth from the right.*

CHAPTER 22

ONE LONG NIGHT

In my early forties, I spent several years working for a defense contractor. I had a coworker at the time named Keith Jolly who was based in the Washington, DC, area, but whom I'd become friends with through work-related travel. Keith had recently started his own company providing endurance events to the public. He told me he was going to be holding an event in Chicago on April 12, 2014, and suggested I participate. I'm typically up for a challenge, so I jumped at the chance.

I invited a couple of friends, Bill and Mick, to join me for this experience. Keith is a former active-duty US Marine, and I soon learned that his idea of an endurance event was much different than a ten-to-twelve-mile Tough Mudder event. For instance, we would be starting the event at 10:00 p.m. on a Friday night and end "sometime on Saturday." This news immediately increased the fear factor!

A relatively small group of us, around fifteen, met at a pub in Chicago for one final meal before we started. We were a mix of men and women from different back-grounds and ranging in age from midtwenties to early for-ties. Some were super fit, but most of us seemed either average or slightly above average. After eating, we all met again at Buckingham Fountain at 10:00 p.m. to start the event. I was a little nervous, but overall confident based on my fitness level at the time and the fact that my good friend Keith was leading us.

We warmed up by doing walking lunges from Buckingham Fountain to a softball field in the adjacent park. When we arrived there, we were told to find someone approximately our own weight. My partner was a 6'3" lanky guy. This first challenge of the night would prove to be perhaps the hardest physical thing I've done in my life to date.

Starting at home plate of the softball diamond, one partner was to lie on his or her back as the other partner straddled them on all fours. The partner lying on their back would then wrap their arms around the neck of the partner on top, clasping their hands together. This position was more than a little awkward with a stranger hovering above me, as I started out on my back.

My partner's job was to bear-crawl around the base paths of the dirt infield while I held onto him, letting my body drag along the ground. I was surprised how quickly and easily my partner made this exercise look. We actually reached home plate before any other group, but now we had to switch places. He got on his back and wrapped his arms around my neck, and I began dragging him from home plate to first base in a bear-crawl position.

Perhaps it was because his long frame created a lot of drag along the base paths, or perhaps it was just because I wasn't in as good a shape as I thought, but I wasn't nearly as good at this challenge as my partner was. I had to take several breaks to catch my breath as I drug him around the bases. My neck was killing me. I was absolutely gassed!

After what seemed like hours, I finally rounded third base. We were still in first place, but another pair was catching up with us due to my lack of speed. The final portion of the drag down the third-base line was miserable. My eyes had trouble focusing, I heaved for air, and it seemed like home plate was getting further away rather than closer. My partner below me encouraged me as best he could, telling me that the other couple was catching up to us. I made a final push as I saw the other couple out of the corner of my eye quickly approaching. With one final effort, I dragged my partner across home plate just in time to claim the victory.

I rolled off my partner onto my back, gasping for air. After a couple of minutes of heaving, I crawled into some grass in foul territory, still working to recover from the misery I'd just endured. It was at this point that my mind started to work against me. I realized that this was only the first event of the night, and it was likely only going to get worse. I began doubting my ability to finish. Sure, I'd brought two buddies along with me, but they'd be fine if I decided to leave early, right? I was already justifying leaving them in my head.

A guy about ten years younger than me, and in seemingly better shape, crawled up into the grass nearby after he and his partner reached home plate. He began losing the meal we'd enjoyed an hour or so earlier. I thought, *If he's having this hard of a time, how the heck am I going to get through this night?* Despite all of the negative thoughts, I somehow convinced myself to stay for the next challenge, just to see how intense it was, before bailing on Bill, Mick, and Keith.

After we left the softball field, we divided into teams that would exist for the remainder of the event. The goal was to try to win "top team" at the end of the event. The next challenge was definitely not as hard as dragging my partner around those base paths. In fact, none of the other challenges were as difficult as that first one had been. After the second challenge, I convinced myself to stay for one more, then one more, then one more after that. I just kept "baby-stepping" my way through.

We were given tasks to complete and checkpoints to reach throughout the night and into the next morning. We ran for miles, did physical conditioning on the sandy beach of Lake Michigan, and even had to strip down and crawl into the cold lake. I later estimated that we covered around twenty miles. We ended in early afternoon Saturday at Navy Pier. My team was fortunate to win enough of the challenges to be named "top team." I give most of the credit to the fact that we had a young lady on our team who later became a champion on another race circuit. She made all of us average Joes much better.

As soon as the event was over and Bill, Mick, and I were waiting for our train to get back to the suburbs, I remember telling them, "There's no way I'd ever do that again." Yet, less than an hour later as we rode the train home and shared stories about our experience, I began thinking that maybe I would do it again. I felt very proud that I hadn't quit and that I had just finished something that many others could not or would not. Yes, Tough Mudder in 2011 boosted my confidence, but this event was like Tough Mudder on steroids for me. I felt like I could have tackled any adversity in that moment.

LESSON

Life is full of choices and chances. Our choices impact

our chances, and the chances we get impact our choices. The better your choices, the better your chances. Every day we have numerous choices to make. We choose to rise early or sleep in. We choose what we'll eat, what tasks we'll work on, and the effort and attitude that we'll have as we do them. Of course, we don't always make the right choices. We're human, after all. But, if we can somehow manage to make the majority of our choices wisely, we improve our chances of happiness, success, fulfillment, and influence.

I had lots of choices to make in regards to the event with Keith. I had the choice to register or not. I had to choose to show up or bail out after I registered. I had to choose multiple times to stay or leave early (quit). I had to choose to be a good teammate or not. I had to make many choices throughout the event about the quality of effort I was going to give to each challenge Keith presented me. I had to choose over and over to have as positive of an attitude as possible to help myself and my teammates.

Because I made mostly good choices during that event, I gave myself a chance to finish. I gave my teammates and myself a chance to be named "top team." I gave myself the chance to gain confidence as a result of what I experienced, and I didn't have to leave with regrets of what could've happened if I'd only chosen differently.

TEAM APPLICATION

Athletes are looking for chances (opportunities), but have they made the necessary amount of good choices that getting a good chance demands?

- Has the athlete made enough good choices over time to earn the chance to start?
- Has the athlete made enough good choices over time to earn the trust of their coaches and teammates?
- Has the athlete made enough good choices over time to earn the grades required to play?
- Has the athlete made enough good choices over time to earn the skills to play at an elite level?

Teams are also looking for chances (i.e. win conference, win regional, win state), but have they collectively made the necessary amount of good choices that getting a good chance demands?

- Have enough members of the team made good enough choices over time to earn the chance to win at the desired level?
- Have the coaches and players made good enough choices over time to build a culture that helps teammates reach their potential?
- Have the leaders of the team made good enough choices over time to positively and effectively lead the team to a good chance?

Principle:
The better my choices, the better my chances.

A photo taken from that night as we ran on Michigan Avenue Beach. I'm the second from the left.

CHAPTER 23

MARATHON

I decided to make 2014 my year of fear. I'd let fear dictate my decisions for far too long and far too often, so I really wanted to focus on doing things that scared me. By doing this, I hoped to be able to lessen the grip of fear in my life. I'd wanted to try working out at a CrossFit gym, but had been too afraid to try, so I did that in 2014. I had always been too afraid to lead a Bible study, so I did that, as well. If I felt fear creep in my head and whisper words that I felt were trying to hold me back, I tried my best to step into that fear.

In my opinion, there are clearly two types of fear. One is good and one is bad. Fear that I call "commonsense fear" is good and helpful to us. Commonsense fear is the fear that tells us to move off the tracks when a train is coming. It's the same fear that prevents us from jumping out of airplanes without parachutes. We must listen to our commonsense fears. They protect us from serious injuries or death.

The other type of fear is what I call "ain't-worth-two-cents fear." Growing up in the South, if something or someone was of little or no value to others, we sometimes would say that thing or person "ain't worth two cents."

Ain't-worth-two-cents fears are of little value to us. They attempt to hold us back from things that might be amazing, if we only had the courage to do or try them. These are the fears that keep us from riding that roller coaster, trying out for the team, trying again when we fail, asking someone to dance, joining that club, asking for the promotion, stepping up to lead, moving to another city, and from registering to run a marathon.

I'd always doubted that I could run a marathon. I had thoughts throughout my adult life that I'd like to try it, but my ain't-worth-two-cents fear did a good job of preventing me from trying. Those fears had even created valid excuses in my head. "I'm a sprinter," I'd say to others. "No way I could train my fast-twitch muscle fibers to run that distance." That's right, I'd tell others that it was a genetic flaw that prevented me from running a marathon. The truth was that I was scared to try. I'd heard how long and miserable the training was. Could I even do it? What if I tried and failed? I wasn't sure my ego could handle that.

In early 2014, a representative from a nonprofit organization visited my church to form a group of us to run the Chicago Marathon that year and raise money for their charity while doing so. I liked the fact that they raised funds to help bring clean drinking water to villages in Africa. I could get on board with that cause. Running a marathon to do it, on the other hand, was a tougher sell. Near the end of the sales pitch, this guy said, "Even Oprah ran the Chicago Marathon."

Wait, what? Now he was just trying to make me look bad! I was in much better physical shape than Oprah, so if she could start and finish a marathon, what was stopping me? Nothing but fear. Since this was my year of fear, I decided to step into that fear.

A group of about fifteen of us registered and started training in April of 2014. The leader of our group had already run marathons, so he helped the rest of us by providing us with a training plan to prepare us for the 26.2-mile marathon. I ran on my own during the week, and we had longer training runs with the group on the weekends.

Training for me was definitely challenging. I was not in great running shape when we started, but thankfully we started with very short runs and just slowly built up our endurance over time. Perhaps the hardest part of training was making the time to do all the training runs, both during the week and on the weekends. I'm married with five very active kids, so there were always plenty of excuses to not make the time to train. But, I really wanted to accomplish running a marathon on my terms—not having to stop and walk along the way. I certainly wanted to finish it better than Oprah did!

About a month before the race, we did our longest training run, which was twenty miles. It was a bear! It was also hot and humid that day, which made it even tougher. But, I did it! I was feeling so confident after that run. I'd never run that far in my life. On race day, I'd just have to find a way to suffer through doing that again and adding another 6.2 miles to the end of it, and I'd be a marathoner!

During the last three weeks of training, our training program called for much shorter runs to allow our bodies to recover and be ready for race day. I was really looking forward to this part of the training. However, during the last three weeks, I began to get horrible cramps in the tibialis muscles, which run up the front of your lower leg along the shin bone. I'd stop and try to stretch the cramps out, but they got so bad I had to quit the training runs soon after I started them. All the confidence I'd built up after that twenty-mile run was now gone. I just knew these cramps would continue into race day and would cause me to quit or have to walk the race. I'd persevered through so many long training runs. I'd invested so much time. I'd made so many personal sacrifices to train, eat, and sleep as I should.

I showed up on race day with little confidence that I'd be able to finish the marathon the way I wanted. I was fairly confident I'd have to walk much of the race, if not quit it altogether. But, I showed up, which is half the battle, they say. I'd raised money for charity, I was part of a team, and I'd certainly worked hard to be there, so at least I could show up. Soon after I arrived to the tent where our team gathered, I was handed a permanent marker and told to write my name in big letters on the front of my running jersey. I did so without asking questions.

As my group approached the starting line on that beautiful October day in Chicago, I was nervously excited, but still doubting myself pretty heavily. I would be keeping pace that day with one of my very best friends (who happens to be my pastor), Jon Peacock. Jon had already run a couple marathons himself, which gave me a sense a security running alongside him.

We crossed the starting line and began running. I felt great initially. Not running much in the last few weeks had my legs feeling pretty fresh. And man, all the people! I heard that there are about 2 million people who line the streets throughout the Chicago Marathon just to cheer for the runners. They hold signs, yell, blow horns and whistles, and ring cowbells. Their energy is amazing! I needed it, because those same familiar cramps started on mile two. The self-doubt crept in. I began to think about stopping to walk a number of times. I wondered if I'd have to quit.

Because I'd written my name on my jersey, I heard my name cheered by the crowd so many times. I heard, "Go, Blake! Keep it up, Blake! Don't stop, Blake! You got this, Blake!" throughout the race.

Despite the cramps, I didn't stop. The energy and encouragement from the crowd wouldn't let me. With people cheering me on, I felt like I could've run fifty miles that day! Eventually, the cramps in my legs went away and didn't return. I certainly felt pain all throughout my legs by the end of the race, but I finished the marathon the way I wanted: without being forced to stop and walk.

LESSON

I learned so much in training for and running a marathon. I certainly had to overcome fear to give myself a chance to be able to become a marathon finisher. I certainly benefitted being surrounded by the "Jimbos" in the crowd who cheered for me. Without them, my experience would've been very different. However, the lesson I want to focus on here is that my goal required me to make sacrifices.

Any goal that really challenges you in some worthwhile way will require that you make sacrifices. To be the best teammate and athlete you can be, you need to be willing to make repeated sacrifices over a long period of time. If your *why* isn't big enough to help you make the decision to do that, you just won't reach your full potential as a teammate or athlete. This scenario leads to a lot of regret and "what could've been" thoughts.

My goal of running the marathon required that I make the following sacrifices repeatedly:

- *Comfort*: I had to sacrifice a whole lot of physical comfort and be willing to make myself very uncomfortable over a five-month training schedule in order to have the best chance of surviving the incredible discomfort I faced on race day. There were many days when I had to sacrifice the comfort of the bed to get in the early morning-run before it got too hot outside. There were plenty of times where I just didn't feel like going on a run, because I knew it would make me uncomfortable, but I had to sacrifice remaining in my comfort zone. I had to sacrifice the comfortable things I wanted in the moment.

- *Time*: Training for a marathon, especially the long runs, requires a lot of time. To set myself up for success, I had to sacrifice a lot of time that I could have used to get more work done, to be with my wife and kids, or to simply get more sleep. On training days, I had even less expendable time to choose to do things that I really enjoy. Had I not been willing to sacrifice time, I wouldn't have been well prepared.

The success that you want in life comes at a price. The problem is that we don't always know the price; we just have to keep sacrificing and putting in the work until we finally achieve our desired success. The journey to success may be longer for some than for others. But, the ones who make more sacrifices than their competition will have the best chance of obtaining the success they want.

TEAM APPLICATION

Great student-athletes are products of great sacrifice, with rare exception. To become exceptionally skilled in a sport requires a great sacrifice in comfort and time on behalf of the student. They've spent many hours and given a lot of sweat to attain their advanced skills. They've even chosen to miss out on some social events in order to get in extra work or play in that tournament.

The parents/guardians of these athletes typically have had to sacrifice greatly, as well. They may have sacrificed a lot financially to pay for lessons, league fees, equipment fees, and maybe even mental coaching. They've sacrificed a large amount of time acting as a taxi for their child, watching practices and games, and washing work-out clothes and uniforms.

Behind every great student-athlete are coaches who helped get them there. Coaches also make tremendous sacrifices for their team and their players. There are long spells during the year when coaches are required to sacrifice a lot of time away from their families and friends in order to serve their student-athletes.

To sacrifice something is to give up something you want—not an easy thing to do once, much less repeatedly over a long period of time. If a team has one player willing to make great sacrifices to become better for the team, the team will get a little better. If a team is filled with athletes willing to make big sacrifices for the sake of the team, then the team's potential goes through the roof.

The hard part is choosing to sacrifice something you want now for something you want in the future (delayed gratification). In the moment, my feelings try to dictate my decisions. My feelings are often focused more on what I want now, instead of what I want in the future. Here are some examples to illustrate:

- In this moment, I feel like eating that package of cookies, but if I choose not to, I am closer to the body I need to perform better in the future.
- In this moment, I feel like staying up late and playing that video game, but if I choose to go to sleep instead, I'll feel better and have more energy at practice tomorrow.
- In this moment, I feel like sleeping late, but if I choose to get up early, I can get in some extra skill work that'll make me a better player when the season starts.
- In this moment, I'd rather watch this TV show instead of going to the gym, but if I sacrifice the TV time, I'll be one small step closer to my dream of making All-Conference.

Principle:
I must sacrifice what I want now
for what I dream of in the future.

My teammates and me (middle of front row) after we completed the 2014 Chicago Marathon (Photo courtesy of Team World Vision)

CHAPTER 24

DISCIPLINE

Instead of making a list of New Year's resolutions each year, I decide on one word that describes an aspect of my life I want to work to improve in the coming year. On December 10, 2018, I decided on the one thing I wanted to focus on improving in 2019: my discipline. I wasn't happy with the way my 2018 ended due to my lack of discipline, especially in the areas of diet and exercise, so I really wanted to focus on improving my discipline in those areas.

Rather than waiting to start improving my discipline on New Year's Day, I thought it would show extra discipline to begin the process the very next day. My plan to show greater discipline in my exercise initially only involved one action: wake up at 5:00 a.m. every day and exercise. Sounds easy, right?

As background, I've never been a wake-up-early-and-work-out guy. In fact, waking up early has always been a very real struggle for me. Once I wake up, I generally come to life fairly quickly, but the first five minutes are an absolute nightmare. At various points of my life I've tried to get up early and work out so that I didn't have to try and find time later in the day to get it done, but the longest streak of days I think I ever had was four. It was just too uncomfortable for me, so I resolved to believe that some people can get up early to work out, and others can't; I'm obviously one of those that can't. I used other excuses, as well, such as, "I just don't feel strong in the morning," and "My body is too stiff to work out in the morning."

Despite my failures to rise early and work out throughout my life, on December 11, 2018, I made yet another attempt to have the discipline to get my workout done before my work and family responsibilities begin. That first 5:00 a.m. wake-up call was hard, but wasn't too tough, because I had some excitement about this new leaf I was turning over. Over the next few days, I continued to repeat the process, waiting for the wake-up time to get easier. It didn't.

I'm now six months into this routine, and I'm still waiting for it to get easy. Guess what? I don't think it will, nor do I think it's supposed to. Sure, some days have been easier than others, but overall, each morning has been an absolute grind to force myself out of bed, make myself presentable, and get to the gym. Though a part of me wishes it would get easier, I know that easy is not what I'm after. Easy doesn't make me better. Easy is for the common man, and I'm demanding uncommon from myself.

One interesting fact about the first ninety days of this lifestyle change is how easily the excuses to sleep in appear, and how attractive they are. In the first ninety days, I was confronted with so many excuses to stray from this discipline commitment I've made. Every single day, there is at least one excuse, but most often there are several. Here's a list of the excuses that tried to entice me to end the streak in the first ninety days, with my response in parentheses:

- "You didn't get enough sleep last night." *(Maybe I can take a nap later. If not, I'll just deal with being a little tired today. Other people deal with much worse each day.)*
- "The bed is so comfortable. Lie back down." *(Hey, bed, I'm not having this conversation with you right now. I'm choosing discipline.)*
- "It's too cold outside. Get back in bed." *(As long as the truck will start, it's warm enough.)*
- "You're way too congested to go to the gym." *(My sinuses don't lift the weights for me, so they don't get a vote.)*
- "There's too much snow on the roads." *(My truck has four-wheel drive, so I'll manage.)*
- "The remote start on the truck doesn't work because of the cold." *(I'll start it by hand then, like most of the people in the world do.)*
- "You're going to have to shovel the driveway before you can leave for the gym." *(Sounds like a pre-workout to my workout this morning. Let's go!)*
- "You have a lot of driving to do today, so a little extra sleep will help." *(Nice try. My workout and proper eating will give me the energy I need for the drive.)*
- "You don't have a gym available today." *(You're right. I'll do burpees in the hotel room instead.)*
- "The hotel gym's door says it doesn't open until 6:00 a.m." *(I'll get up and try it anyway to see if I'm able to get in.)*
- "Your muscles are too sore to get up and work out today." *(I'll at least do a little something and visit the hot tub to help the muscles recover.)*

- "You've got a strained muscle in your back." *(I'll stick with exercises that don't hurt that muscle.)*
- "Sore throat today, so you must be getting sick." *(There's a difference between getting sick and being sick. I'll show up and see what I can do.)*
- "Your body could use an off day." *(I don't take off days, but maybe I'll just do some stretching and walk on the treadmill to allow my body to recover.)*
- "You have an early commitment tomorrow, so you won't be able to get up at 5:00 a.m. and get in a workout." *(You're right. I'll get up at 4:30 instead.)*

I imagine you've heard many of these excuses yourself, or at least ones that sound a lot like them. These excuses seem so evil to me. Why is it that they call me toward comfort? They try to keep me from improving myself. They're not looking out for my best interests. They're like an anchor that wants to drag along the bottom of the ocean to keep my boat from speeding ahead.

Discipline is the hard choice, but it is a choice. The most powerful tool God gave us, in my opinion, is the power to choose. I can choose the excuse, or I can choose discipline. I then deal with the consequences either way. I'm trying to sacrifice the things I want now (i.e. comfort, sleep, junk food, etc.) for the things I want most later. It's really a practice in delayed gratification. I can have the things I want now and be left unsatisfied with my level of fitness, or I can sacrifice those things and invest in a sometimes slow, laborious process of achieving the fitness level I dream of.

At the time of writing this, the streak is only two hundred days long. If you ever see me, I welcome you to ask me if the streak is still alive. I'd love to one day be able to say that I've been getting up at 5:00 a.m. for twenty consecutive years, but I know I can only do that by finding a way to get up again tomorrow.

LESSON

A few years ago, I read a story about a woman who swam from Cuba to Florida. She tried and failed on four different occasions, learning a lesson from each attempt that would help her in the future. On her fifth attempt, in 2013, she had a motto that she repeated to herself while she swam. The motto was "Find a way." On that attempt, she indeed found a way to complete the swim, becoming the first woman to swim that stretch of water without a shark cage.

Since hearing this story, I've been trying to live by those words as much as possible. You see, I believe there are two types of people in this world: those who find a way, and those who find an excuse. Which one are you going to be? Which one am I going to be? I've certainly been a "find-an-excuse guy" for much of my life, but now I try to find a way to get things done. I try to find a way to be positive. I try to find a way to see the opportunities in life. I try to find a way to live up to the people and things I've committed to.

You likely know someone who seems to always have an excuse when they fall short. They have an excuse for everything! Maybe that describes you. If it does, I'd like to challenge you to turn over a new leaf and pursue the find-a-way lifestyle.

TEAM APPLICATION

I have been on and worked with teams where I could easily spot the teammates prone to finding excuses. They can give you an excuse for:

- Why they're late
- Why they don't have their equipment
- Why they have to miss practice
- Why they're not a starter
- Why they weren't chosen to be team captain
- Why they're not in better shape
- Why they didn't make the play

These players drove me nuts when I played with them, and they still drive me nuts. Just take ownership of your mistake already! We all make mistakes, but we all don't take responsibility for them.

Coaches and teammates can see through excuses. Players who continually give excuses for not living up to the required standards of behavior for the team lose trust. And, players who can't be trusted by their team spend more time on the bench than they do in the game. Players who can be trusted more get more playing time.

Principle:
I will find a way, not an excuse.

ABOUT THE AUTHOR

Blake Williams is the founder and president of Battle-Tested, a nonprofit organization focused on helping student-athletes prepare for the battles they will face in life, both on and off the field. He's facilitated hundreds of events for thousands of high school and college student-athletes that challenge them physically, mentally, and morally. Blake also serves as a mental performance coach to help student-athletes overcome the mental challenges that can limit their performance on the field, and the moral challenges that can limit their effectiveness in the locker room.